More praise for *Rooted*....

"*Rooted* is ancient medicine for the ailing North American church. Cannata and Reitano don't just cynically decry the modern Christian's failure to know what they believe and why they believe it—they offer an antidote in the time-tested wisdom of the Apostle's Creed."

Ray Cortese
Senior Pastor
Seven Rivers Presbyterian Church, Crystal
River, FL

"Cannata and Reitano's book on the Apostle's Creed is crucially important at this time for Christians in America. As the baptismal creed of the early Church (the creed that people had to confess at baptism and thus for entry into the Church), it lays out with utmost concision and clarity what C. S. Lewis memorably called "mere Christianity." Unfortunately, in this day, mere Christianity is not good enough for many professing Christians. Fundamentalists, who like everything spelled out in terms of a naive biblicism, see in the Apostle's creed too much latitude for legitimate Christian faith. And theological liberals, who hate the encumbrances of doctrines that might put them at odds with the reigning secular ideologies (doctrines such as the Virgin Birth, Hell, and Judgment), see in the Apostle's creed outdated dogmas that no right-thinking contemporary Christians ought to accept. In response to these two polarizing streams, Cannata and Reitano's book provides a much needed corrective. They brilliantly explain each of the key statements of this creed, their explanations being rooted at once in classical Christian orthodoxy, but also brought up to date by addressing current challenges to the Christian faith. Mere Christianity is under threat."

William A. Dembski
Senior fellow with Discovery Institute's
Center for Science and Culture
Author, The Design Revolution

"The authors analyze the Apostles Creed in a manner that is simultaneously scholarly and entertaining. Dr. Cannata's and Rev. Reitano's backgrounds as church planters, a church historian, and a performance entertainer blend together in the unfolding of this valuable text. They take an ancient cliche document and bring it to life for a 21st century population, both of believers and those who are seeking the gift of faith."

Richard Gardiner, Ph.D.
History Education Professor
Columbus State University, Columbus, GA

"In *Rooted*, Cannata and Reitano have created a valuable guide that unpacks the Apostles' Creed for a contemporary audience. They draw upon church Fathers and Reformers, as well as current evangelical leaders, to explain and apply the Creed to our lives in ways that are immediately practical and pastoral. The combination of scripture, stories, sermons, and insights, together with study questions after each chapter, makes for an accessible and useful text for Christians young and old, both new converts and those who have confessed the Creed for decades."

Joel Garver
Assistant Professor of Philosophy
La Salle University, Philadelphia, PA

"Christian, what do you believe? 1800 years ago, Christians summarized their answer to this question in what has come to be known as the Apostles' Creed. Written in an engaging style, Cannata and Reitano explain its continuing relevance in *Rooted: The Apostles' Creed*. Their careful yet lively analysis describes the meaning and significance of the creed for individual Christians and the church at large today."

P.C. Kemeny
Professor of Religion and Humanities
Grove City College, Grove City, PA

"I love this book and will use it in the pulpit and classroom alike, along with my own journey with Christ. It isn't often that scholarship, relevance, humor and pastoral warmth converge in the same book, but thanks to the authors' careful treatment and shepherding instincts, they have done so in *Rooted*. It was difficult to put the book down because Ray and Josh were able to take the reader back to the conflicts and passions that drove the writing of this magnificent Creed, while capturing the heart of the gospel: "The Christian story is ultimately hopeful." It makes this ancient document very 'human,' and for this, I am in their debt."

Mike Khandjian
Senior Pastor
Chapelgate Presbyterian Church, Baltimore, MD

"In a day and age of 'cafeteria style' Christianity where 'whatever works for you' is championed and the hard won-faith of our fathers is often neglected if not outright ignored, it's refreshing to see this work by Ray Cannata & Josh Reitano.
"The 'make it up as you go along' approach that has been utilized by some of the present day manifestations of the Church attempting to be relevant has resulted in a certain losing of the baby with the bath water. Such strains of the faith often lose the richness of the Creed's evangelical heritage. Under this quick rush to be relevant & innovative, the Apostle's Creed, which has united almost all of Christendom for 2000 years, has (sadly) often gone missing in action.
"Enter Cannata & Reitano. C.S.Lewis has said that perhaps the best poet is more like a theologian at the top of his game; and likewise, a great theologian, when in top form is closer to the spirit of a poet. I get that same sense from the authors among these pages.
"The authors argue that the Creed, by reinforcing the non-negotiables of 'the faith once for all delivered to the saints,' reminds us in not only of 'the best story there has ever been,' but it also of it's continued immediacy & relevancy now. Further, the Creed calls us to a community where our new found identity is nurtured, grown and sustained.
"Written in a non-academic and readable style, Ray & Josh highlight this non-static, dynamic, 'present-ness' of the Creed. They call us to reckon the nearness of the Lord

to Whom the Creed has precisely testified to for centuries. The Church has, as one of her treasures, a Creed that succinctly declares that God, as Creator, Redeemer and Rebuilder of the world through His Spirit in the Church, is very much with us indeed!

"The Creed thus bears precise testimony the Father who loves us and is inexorably committed to us."

Bill Malonee
Musician, Vigilantes of Love
(named one of Paste magazine's top 100
songwriters of all time)

"The fierce winds and rains of Hurricane Katrina exposed the weak substructures of physical levees and social systems corroded by injustice and neglect. But, most of the majestic, aged oak trees of Audubon Park and the Gulf Coast still stand today, because they are deeply and widely *Rooted*. With this book, Ray Cannata and Josh Reitano explore a root system that has provided strength enough for the church to withstand the winds of adversity across cultures and centuries. This study of the Apostles Creed will not only strengthen your church family's root system in worship and fellowship, it will help equip you and your congregation for the crosswinds of intergenerational, intercultural mission."

Dr. Gregory Perry
Associate Professor of New Testament &
Director of the City Ministry Initiative
Covenant Theological Seminary, St Louis,
MO

"Cannata and Reitano bring the Apostles' Creed to life as a tried and tested source of lived wisdom for Christians. But *Rooted: the Apostles' Creed* is much more than merely an illuminating exposition of the Creed. It offers an engaging exploration of the plot and logic of the Christian theological tradition and challenges readers to root their daily lives in such realities. Rich in pastoral insight and readily accessible to a broad readership, this book should become a very popular resource among churches committed to the theological formation of their members."

David Riggs
Associate Professor of History & Executive
Director of John Wesley Honors College
Indiana Wesleyan University, Marion, IN

"Ray and Josh know where they come from and this book is like being led back to your hometown and reminded of the experiences and realities that shaped your life."

Shayne Wheeler
Author, The Briarpatch Gospel: Fearlessly
Following Jesus Into the Thorny Places
Lead Pastor
All Souls Fellowship, Decatur, GA

ROOTED

ROOTED

THE APOSTLES' CREED

RAYMOND F. CANNATA

JOSHUA D. REITANO

Rooted: the Apostles' Creed

Published by:

Doulos Resources, 1506 N Highland Avenue, Murfreesboro, TN 37130; PHONE: (901) 201-4612 WEBSITE: www.doulosresources.org.

Please address all questions about rights and reproduction to Doulos Resources: PHONE: (901) 201-4612; E-MAIL: info@doulosresources.org.

Published 2013

Printed in the United States of America by Ingram/Lightning Source

ISBNs:

978-1-937063-92-4 (print)

978-1-937063-91-7 (digital)

Library of Congress Control Number: 2013949127

Cover design by Kristin Boys, 2013.

This book is printed using paper that is produced according to Sustainable Forestry Initiative® (SFI®) Certified Sourcing.

Doulos Resources
www.doulosresources.org

FOR ANDREW & RACHEL, PAIGE & LUCY

CONTENTS

Preface

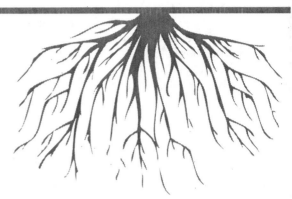

This work is the product of a long process of seeking to understand and apply God's Word through the categories of the Creed.

It began in 2005, when Rev. Matthew Brown was planting a young church in Park Slope, Brooklyn and I (Ray) was pastor of an established sister church in suburban New Jersey. For a couple of years Matt and I had been writing our sermons together each week, using the same texts and conferring by email and phone. Together we developed a series on the Apostles' Creed in an attempt to root our congregation in the great ecumenical doctrines of the faith. We hoped that these tested truths would help build a foundation from which our church could move out to serve in mission to our neighbors.

Several years later, I was re-planting a newer church in New Orleans. Our young congregation included many with little background in Christianity. In the aftermath of Hurricane Katrina we struggled to know how to ground our mission to our neighborhood. I returned to these old sermons Matt and I had written a few years earlier. I found that in most cases my older sermons were not fully adequate for this new context, and I significantly altered or completely re-wrote each of them.

A few years later my friend Rev. Joshua Reitano was planting a new church in Cincinnati, and also looked to the Creed as a useful tool to help his young congregation put down roots for mission. I sent him my sermons as idea starters. Several of them proved helpful as he adapted the themes to his own neighborhood context, thought, and style. For other articles of the Creed he chose to start fresh and take his messages in entirely different directions.

In 2011 we decided to share some of the things God's Word had taught us in these exercises by editing Josh's sermon texts for book form.

Anyone who has preached knows that citing all of your smaller sources in a sermon produces much tedious detail that most listeners find distracting and pointless. And even when acknowledgments are made orally, most preachers tend not to record all of this in their sermon notes. Josh and I each preach about 500 manuscript pages per year (175,000 words each!) and do not usually footnote our sources. While we have made great efforts to track down as many of our sources as possible for adapting these messages to book form, I fear we likely missed a few. We sincerely apologize to any who may not be fully credited, but we tried our best.

In addition to the various biblical commentaries that we used for our texts, the books on the Creed that we found most useful include: Luke Timothy Johnson (2003), Roger Van Harn (2004), and Alister McGrath (1997).

Ray Cannata
July 14 (Bastille Day), 2011

The Apostles' Creed

I believe in God the Father Almighty,
Maker of heaven and earth.
I believe in Jesus Christ, his only Son, our Lord,
who was conceived by the Holy Spirit, and born
     of the virgin Mary.
He suffered under Pontius Pilate,
was crucified, died, and was buried;
he descended into Hell.[1]
The third day he rose again from the dead.
He ascended into heaven
and is seated at the right hand of God the
     Father Almighty.
From there he will come to judge the living and
     the dead.
I believe in the Holy Spirit,
the holy catholic church,
the communion of saints,
the forgiveness of sins,
the resurrection of the body,
and the life everlasting.
Amen.

---

1 Some churches translate this phrase "he descended to the dead."

I Believe in God the Father Almighty

CHAPTER 1

¹The heavens declare
  the glory of God,
and the sky above proclaims
  his handiwork.
²Day to day pours out speech,
and night to night reveals knowledge.
³There is no speech, nor are there words,
whose voice is not heard.
⁴Their voice goes out through all the earth,
and their words to the end of the world.
In them he has set a tent for the sun,
⁵which comes out like a bridegroom leaving his chamber,
and, like a strong man, runs its course with joy.
⁶Its rising is from the end of the heavens,
and its circuit to the end of them,
and there is nothing hidden from its heat.
⁷The law of the LORD is perfect,
reviving the soul;
the testimony of the LORD is sure,
making wise the simple...

Psalm 19

I (Ray) don't know what your experience in kindergarten was like, but I bet it wasn't so different from mine at Public School 8 in New York City. There was a lot of diversity in my school: smart kids; not so smart kids; different ethnicities; different sizes; the kids who ate paste and the kids who didn't. And at P.S. 8 everybody (no matter who they were) fought on the playground. But one thing brought us all together: the Pledge of Allegiance. That was a unifying exercise, even in all our diversity.

It doesn't take great powers of observation to see that the church resembles my kindergarten class at P.S. 8. There is great variety in the church: Eastern Orthodox, Roman Catholics, Baptists, Pentecostals, Methodists, Lutherans, Presbyterians; some who eat paste and some who don't. Every denomination has its strengths and weaknesses, as well as its unique history and traditions. Sometimes Christians get into fights like kids on the playground. But there is one thing that has united Christians from every tradition: the Apostles' Creed.

A legend developed by the turn of the 5th century that attributed each clause of the Apostles' Creed to one of Jesus' disciples. Supposedly, the twelve apostles were gathered and preparing for their mission, and Peter (as usual) spoke first and said, "I believe in God the Father Almighty, Maker of heaven and earth." And then Andrew chimed in, "yes, and in Jesus Christ his only Son, our Lord." And so on.

It's a nice story, but that's not how it happened. The Apostles' Creed developed early in the history of Christianity, as the fledgling faith began to grow and spread beyond the bounds of Judaism. Hebrew converts, for the most part, needed to be taught that Jesus was the Messiah promised in the Old Testament. But many Gentiles were coming to believe in Christ, and the church needed a way to explain its most important doctrines.

And so the Apostles' Creed was developed, with early drafts being used before AD 200. By the 500s the Creed was in its final form. And though it was not written by the Apostles, it was meant to summarize their teaching.[2]

Before we dig too much into the heart of the Creed, it's important to make some comments on the nature of creeds in general.

"I Believe"

A creed is a simple of statement of fundamental beliefs. We might think of the Apostles' Creed as the Christian Pledge of Allegiance, uniting Christians. But it also can also be the source of controversy.

Creeds are Inevitable

Can a modern person really subscribe to a creed? It seems rather narrow, and probably a bit unsophisticated. Shouldn't you have an open mind? Shouldn't you be your own person? In the modern world, belief in a creed is considered a sign of intellectual failure. You can't be bound by a creed, so it is said, and be a truly critical thinker.

Nietzsche speaks for our age when he distinguishes those who *inquire* from those who *believe*. People who inquire are good thinkers; people who believe are simplistic. Nietzsche explains, "in the Christian world of ideas there is nothing that has the least contact with reality—and it is in the instinctive hatred of reality that we recognize the only motivating force at the root of Christianity."[3]

Is Nietzsche correct? Is confessing a creed tantamount to intellectual suicide? A lot of people think so. In the *New York Times Review of Books* there was an article

---

2 For more on the development of the Creed, see Luke Timothy Johnson, *The Creed: What Christians Believe and Why it Matters* (New York, NY: Doubleday, 2003), 11-59.

3 Nietzsche, *The Antichrist*, 39, cited in Johnson, *The Creed* (2003), 2.

called "Down There on a Visit." The writer took a trip to the South where he
kept running into Christians.

> Skepticism, empirical evidence, and book learning are in low esteem
> among the Protestant evangelicals...They reject modern science, and
> they dream of a theocratic state where such blasphemous subject matter
> would be left out from the school curriculum...[4]

For many in the modern world, to be a Christian is a sign of intellectual lazi-
ness or psychological weakness. We have no interest in defending all Christians
everywhere; no doubt there are many who haven't thought about what they believe and why they believe it. But this common criticism directed at Christians
is often that to believe *in anything*, to subscribe to *any set of beliefs*, is ridiculous in
and of itself. To confess the Apostles' Creed is to give away your mind. The next
time you hear that, you might point out that life is not possible without some
form of creed. *Creeds are inevitable.* Whether you are religious or not, everyone
has a creed.

Steve Turner is a British music journalist who has written books about U2,
the Beatles, and Johnny Cash. He is also a poet whose poem "Creed" spoofs mo-
dernity's "creed of creedlessness."

> We believe in marxfreudanddarwin
> We believe everything is ok
> as long as you don't hurt anyone,
> to the best of your definition of hurt,
> and to the best of your knowledge.
> We believe everything's getting better,
> despite evidence to the contrary.
> The evidence must be investigated.
> You can prove anything with evidence.
> We believe that all religions are basically the same.
> They all believe in love and goodness.
> They only differ on matters of
> Creation, sin, heaven, hell, God and salvation.
> We believe that man is essentially good.
> It's only his behavior that lets him down.
> This is the fault of society.
> Society is the fault of conditions.
> Conditions are the fault of society.
> We believe that each man must find the truth that is right for him.
> We believe there is no absolute truth,
> except the truth that there is no absolute truth.
> We believe in the rejection of creeds,

---

4 Charles Simic, "Down There on a Visit," *New York Times Review of Books* (Vol. 51, No. 13; Aug
12, 2004).

and the flowering of individual thought.[5]

Turner nails it. Even the most secular of people have their own sacred beliefs, their inherited creeds, even if they happen to be self-contradictory. Creeds are necessary; they are how we make sense of reality. Everyone interprets life through the lens of some set of basic beliefs.

Atheist Thomas Kuhn in *The Structure of Scientific Revolutions* conclusively demonstrates that modern science is built not on empirical evidence, but on unprovable statements. Even science, to conduct experiments, needs to operate according to untestable presuppositions before it can move forward. The question isn't, "should you have a creed?" but, "what creed should you subscribe to?"

Creeds are Useful

Though creeds are inevitable, the church did not simply adopt theirs by default. The Apostles' Creed was purposefully created to bring people together. The Creed was not meant to be a philosophical defense of the faith, but a lean summary of what all Christians believe. This is helpful because, as you know, the Bible is a long book. The Creed takes the million-word Bible and boils it down to its essence. It's the SparkNotes of the biblical story.

And it is a story, the story of God and his world, complete with characters and a plot. It tells us about the way God interacts with his people. And it tells us about the future. The Creed's story begins with God's creation, and ends with eternity. The plot includes God becoming man. The crisis is Jesus' suffering and death. The resolution is in his resurrection, ascension, and the coming of the Holy Spirit to equip the church to live faithfully until the resurrection of the dead.

When Christians affirm their faith by saying the Apostles' Creed, they are effectively retelling this story. We are summarizing what we believe. But we are also telling one another a story that we already know and often forget. It is a story that bears repeating because there is no better story. And it gives us our bearings in life.

By making explicit what we do believe, the Apostles' Creed also guards the church against what we don't believe. The Creed allows Christians to identify and avoid inadequate or harmful versions of the story.

It also keeps us from riding our own hobby horses by keeping the biblical story in balance. For example, Christians in the western world today tend to be very individualistic. We don't seem to have much of a sense of belonging to a community. Our relationship with God, we think, is only about personal salvation. The Apostles' Creed guards against individualism by reminding us that belonging to the church (and being in community with one another) isn't just *helpful* to the Christian life, it's the *goal* of the Christian life. When we confess

5 Steve Turner, "Creed," originally printed in his book *Nice and Nasty* (London: Marshall, Morgan, and Scott, 1980). Quoted by Ravi Zacharias in *Can Man Live Without God?* (Nashville, TN: Thomas Nelson, 1994), 42-44.

"I believe in the holy catholic (universal) church, and the communion of saints" we are reminded that Christianity is not "just me and Jesus." We are reminded that Jesus died to save a *people* for himself. And he saves us not just out of sin, but into a community. This is not only a local community comprised of people we know, but a global community that transcends times. Despite their differences, Christians throughout the centuries and across the continents have agreed on the tenets of the Apostles' Creed.

There is something beautiful and extraordinary about knowing that when you confess the Apostles' Creed, there are people all over the world doing the same thing in different languages. Swedish Lutherans and Korean Presbyterians, African Pentecostals and Guatemalan Catholics, Chinese house churches and Egyptian Copts — all can affirm, "this is what we believe."

"I Believe in God the Father"

The Apostles' Creed begins with the affirmation "I believe in God the Father." During my (Josh's) years in campus ministry in the Midwest, I met very few students who would deny this statement. The problem came when we tried to clarify what was meant by "God."

It reminds us of a story about Jonathan Edwards. Edwards was a pastor in Massachusetts in the 18th century. After talking about the need for revival in his hometown, an incredulous church member questioned him. "Surely everyone believes in God already?" "Yes," Edwards replied, "but what kind of God do they believe in? When I show them the God of the Bible, they say, 'no, I don't believe in that God. I believe in a God who is more to my liking.'"

Today, many people still believe in God, but there are almost as many definitions of God as there are people who confess belief in him. But the Bible tells us that God is knowable, that he has a true and objective character that does not change. He is our Father. What implications might that have for us?

The Father of Creation

First, it means that we believe that God is the Father of all creation. Psalm 19 displays God as the ultimate author and sustainer of the cosmos. He is the one from whom all things come, the one who generates all things.[6]

> ¹The heavens declare the glory of God,
>   and the sky above proclaims his handiwork.
> ²Day to day pours out speech,
>   and night to night reveals knowledge.
> ³There is no speech, nor are there words,
>   whose voice is not heard.
> ⁴Their voice goes out through all the earth,
>   and their words to the end of the world.

---

6 See Richard A. Norris, Jr., in Regoer E. Van Harn, *Exploring and Proclaiming the Apostles'*

The created world sings of the Maker. The voice rings out through all of creation — God exists! He made all things. And he's glorious in his creativity and might.

This is something that even secular scientists are observing. Australian astrophysicist Paul Davis writes, "The equations of physics have in them incredible simplicity, elegance and beauty. That in itself is sufficient to prove to me that there must be a God who is responsible for these laws and responsible for the universe."[7] Likewise, Arno Penzias, Nobel laureate and the former head of Bell Labs, states, "Astronomy leads us to a unique event, a universe which was created out of nothing and delicately balanced to provide exactly the conditions required to support life. In the absence of an absurdly improbable accident, the observations of modern science seem to suggest an underlying, one might say, supernatural, plan."[8]

Neither of these scientists are professing Christians (so far as we know) but they are sensing the truth of Psalm 19. "The heavens declare the glory of God, and the sky above proclaims his handiwork." All creation bears the mark of its Father, who designed it. The word David uses in verse 1 that we translate as "declare" is a participle in its original Hebrew. The most literal translation would be something like "The heavens *are declaring*." They are telling. They are showing their Father's hand.

Verse 2 says that, day to day, creation "pours out" speech. In Hebrew, the verb means to "bubble up." Day after day, information about God bubbles up out of the created universe. It reminds us of *The Three Stooges*: Larry, Moe, and Curly seem to do a lot of plumbing in that show. In one episode Curly twisted a pipe and water began to shoot out everywhere. He put his hand on it to plug the leak, only to have it shoot from somewhere else. Finally he put both hands on the two leaks only to have water shoot him right in the face.

This is the image in Psalm 19; knowledge about the existence of God is streaming forth from creation, and when we try and plug it, it just bubbles up from somewhere else. We can try to repress this knowledge, but ultimately it is futile. The cosmos sings out the glory of the Maker. The Father is speaking to us in the created world.

God in Three Persons

But to say "I believe in God the Father" means something even more than understanding God to be the creator of the universe. It also subtly underscores that God exists in three persons; when we call God "Father," we are acknowledging his Trinitarian nature.

Creed (Grand Rapids, MI: Wm. B. Eerdmans, 2004), 24; cf. I Corinthians 8:6.

7 Paul Davies, *Superforce* (Austin: Touchstone, 1984).

8 Arno Penzias in Henry Morgenau and Roy Abraham Varghese, eds., *Cosmos, Bios, and Theos* (La Salle, IL: Open Court, 1992), 83.

Jesus referred to God as his Father, which was downright shocking to his contemporaries (John 5:18). Jesus said that the Son loves the Father (John 14:31), he always does what pleases the Father (John 8:29), and that when people look at him, they can know what the Father is like (John 14:9).

Our Father

But the really good news is that it's not only Jesus who can call God "Father." You are invited to call him Father too. Through Jesus, you can become part of God's family. "But to all who did receive [Jesus], who believed in his name, he gave the right to become children of God" (John 1:12). This is called adoption.

Both of our churches have borne witness to many adoptions. This is thrilling, not only because Christians are living out their calling to care for the least and the lost (James 1:27), but also because this is a picture of God's adopting love for us.

You may have heard that Jesus calls God "Abba" (daddy) several times in the New Testament (Mark 14:36, for example). But it's not just Jesus who can do that. The New Testament says that *you* can use this name for God as well. The Apostle Paul reminds Christians in Romans 8:15 that we "did not receive the spirit of slavery to fall back into fear, but you have received the Spirit of adoption as sons, by whom we cry, 'Abba! Father!'" For some of you, this is easy to imagine because you have had great fathers, men who modeled God's compassion and tenderness to you. For others this is more difficult because your experience with your father has not been good.

Henry Lyte was one such unfortunate child. A songwriter, he wrote several of the hymns still used widely in churches, including "Praise My Soul the King of Heaven." Henry had a terrible father. His parents split up and sent him to boarding school. His father later remarried, and from then on wouldn't allow Henry to call him "father" anymore; he signed his letters *"your uncle."* This was terribly hurtful, as you can imagine. But the fatherhood of God became a source of comfort for Henry. In his hymns, he addressed God as his loving Father. He wrote words like:

> "Father-like he tends and spares us;
> Well our feeble frame he knows,
> In His hands He gently bears us,
> Rescues us from all our foes."[9]

The gospel was able to rewrite Henry Lyte's life story. Rather than being defined by an awful earthly father, his life was determined by a wonderful and loving eternal Father.[10]

Notice one other thing. The Apostles' Creed says, "I believe *in* God the Father Almighty." Not "I believe *that* God exists." It is something more than that. When you believe *in* something, it is more than just intellectual assent. It's not

---

9 Henry Lyte, "Praise, My Soul, the King of Heaven."

10 Kevin Twit tells this story about Lyte on the Indelible Grace album, *The Hymn Sing: Live in Nashville*, track 8.

academic. It's not just information. When you believe *in* something, it involves hope and trust."

As you read this, do you believe *that* God exists, or do you believe *in* God the Father? Do you trust him? Do you belong to him? Have you given your life to him?

"I Believe in God the Father Almighty"

The Creed confesses "I believe in God the Father Almighty." William Barclay rightly says the word "almighty" should dispel any tendency toward a sentimental, domesticated Deity.[12] The God Christians confess is God Almighty!

When Christians confess this clause of the Creed, they are calling attention to the fact that God is Lord and King, sovereign and omnipotent. He reigns over the earth. But to call God "almighty" does cause problems for some. J.I. Packer says, "Men treat God's sovereignty as a theme for controversy, but in Scripture it is a matter of worship." Think of the kid trying to stump his Sunday school teacher, asking, "If God can do anything, can he make a rock so big that he can't lift it?" Or, "can God make a square circle?" The short answer to these questions is, "of course not." When the Creed says God is almighty, it is using biblical language that means God can do everything in accordance with his own nature. The Bible is clear that God cannot lie, he cannot cease to be God, or add a fourth member to the Trinity. To call God "almighty" is to say he can do everything that is consistent with who he is.

God is able to do everything he intends to do. And what he intends to do is consistent with his nature. Where do we find that? Psalm 19:7 says: "The law of the Lord is perfect, reviving the soul; the testimony of the Lord is sure, making wise the simple…" When the psalmist is talking about the "law," the testimony, the precepts, he's not merely referring to the Ten Commandments. He is talking in shorthand about the whole Word of God. He's telling us that God's testimony is sure, and nothing he has promised will be withheld from his people. Even when the fulfillment of his promises seems impossible to us, they are always possible for him. As a matter of fact, he seems to enjoy working in surprising ways.

In the Gospel of Luke, we learn about the angel Gabriel coming to visit Mary. He tells her that she is going to give birth to the Savior of the world, to which she replies, "How will this be, since I am a virgin?" That is a legitimate question. Gabriel replies, "Nothing will be impossible with God" (Luke 1:26ff).

If you believe in God the Father Almighty, then you must believe that his testimony is sure and altogether righteous and true. And if that is true, it gives you incredible power to believe and trust in God when trouble comes your way. You can believe that God is mighty to pay the bills in your house, that he can

11 See further Norris in Van Harn, *Exploring and Proclaiming the Apostles' Crreed*, 22-23.

12 William Barclay, *The Apostles' Creed* (Philadelphia, PA: Westminster John Knox Press, 1998), 35.

rescue you from yourself and your long-besetting struggles. You can believe that God can give you peace and joy, even when the world around you doesn't look anything like the Kingdom and doesn't seem to be getting better very quickly. You can believe that God is mighty to guide you as you go out and recklessly pursue his mission to love and serve your neighbors, even when the mission seems impossible. You can believe that God is mighty enough for you to put aside your obsession with being "safe" and move toward the pain of those in need.

Most of all, God is mighty to save, and he does so by keeping his promises in Jesus Christ. Through Jesus' death and resurrection, God the Father is restoring all things, and putting his might on display for all to see.

Where does he reveal his might? More than anywhere else, he reveals it in the cross. At the cross of Jesus Christ, we see God's promises fulfilled. The Almighty God, the omnipotent Ruler, the Lord of All, comes as a humble servant to save his people and to keep his promise. He answers evil with good, persecution with service, hatred with love. His might is displayed in the love of the one who died even for those who sought his death.[13]

You may be in some grim situations right now. Maybe you feel trapped, alone — at work, in your family, in your job. But the cross screams out to you: God's love and power are relentless. He will not stop until he redeems a people for himself. He will not stop until evil is driven from creation and every tear of the redeemed is wiped away. Belief in a God like this revives the soul, and even gives us the boldness to go out fearlessly in mission to serve the world as he has.

---

13 See Colin Gunton in Van Harn, *Exploring and Proclaiming the Apostles' Crreed*, 36.

STUDY QUESTIONS:

- Can a modern person really subscribe to a creed? Do you agree with some that this makes you "closed minded" or inherently "simplistic?" What do you think of the assertion that creeds are inevitable?

- How are creeds used in your church? Do they play a role in worship or in selecting leadership? How can creeds be potentially useful in your life, and in the shared life of your church?

- Creeds often divide Christians. How can they unite them?

- If the whole created world sings of the Maker, what does that say about how we treat others? What does that say about the value of our neighbors, even those who don't yet believe in Christ? What does it say about the value of the environment?

- If the whole of the created world sings of its Maker, why aren't more people able to hear it?

- Some of you had difficult fathers growing up. How does knowing God as Father redefine your notions of fatherhood? How does it change your self-identity? For those of you who are dads, how does this practically impact your approach to parenting?

- If God the Father is "almighty," what does that mean for your day-to-day life? What does it mean when troubles strike? When your relationships seem in danger? When you struggle with failure?

- If God the Father is truly "almighty," why are we so often afraid to boldly pursue the mission of every Christian to move toward pain? How can trusting anew that God is almighty give us the boldness to live with more "danger" for the sake of our mission to serve our neighbors?

Maker of Heaven and Earth

CHAPTER 2

¹In the beginning, God created the heavens and the earth. ²The earth was without form and void, and darkness was over the face of the deep. And the Spirit of God was hovering over the face of the waters.
³And God said, "let there be light," and there was light. ⁴And God saw that the light was good. And God separated the light from the darkness. ⁵God called the light Day, and the darkness he called Night. And there was evening and there was morning, the first day.
⁶And God said, "let there be an expanse in the midst of the waters, and let it separate the waters from the waters." ⁷And God made the expanse and separated the waters that were under the expanse from the waters that were above the expanse. And it was so. ⁸And God called the expanse Heaven. And there was evening and there was morning, the second day.
⁹And God said, "let the waters under the heavens be gathered together into one place, and let the dry land appear." And it was so. ¹⁰God called the dry land Earth, and the waters that were gathered together he called Seas. And God saw that it was good.
¹¹And God said, "let the earth sprout vegetation, plants yielding seed, and fruit trees bearing fruit in which is their seed, each according to its kind, on the earth." And it was so. ¹²The earth brought forth vegetation, plants yielding seed according to their own kinds, and trees bearing fruit in which is their seed, each according to its kind. And God saw that it was good. ¹³And there was evening and there was morning, the third day.
¹⁴And God said, "let there be lights in the expanse of the heavens to separate the day from the night. And let them be for signs and for seasons, and for days and years, ¹⁵and let them be lights in the expanse of the heavens to give light upon the earth." And it was so. ¹⁶And God made the two great lights — the greater light to rule the day and the lesser light to rule the night — and the stars. ¹⁷And God set them in the expanse of the heavens to give light on the earth, ¹⁸to rule over the day and over the night, and to separate the light from the darkness. And God saw that it was good. [19] And there was evening and there was morning, the fourth day.
²⁰And God said, "let the waters swarm with swarms of living creatures, and let birds fly above the earth across the expanse of the heavens." ²¹So God created the great sea creatures and every living creature that moves, with which the waters swarm, according to their kinds, and every winged bird according to its kind. And God saw that it was good. ²²And God blessed them, saying, "be fruitful and multiply and fill the waters in the seas, and let birds multiply on the earth." ²³And there was evening and there was morning, the fifth day.

[24]And God said, "let the earth bring forth living creatures according to their kinds — livestock and creeping things and beasts of the earth according to their kinds." And it was so. [25]And God made the beasts of the earth according to their kinds and the livestock according to their kinds, and everything that creeps on the ground according to its kind. And God saw that it was good.

[26]Then God said, "let us make man in our image, after our likeness. And let them have dominion over the fish of the sea and over the birds of the heavens and over the livestock and over all the earth and over every creeping thing that creeps on the earth."

[27]So God created man in his own image,
in the image of God he created him;
male and female he created them.

[28]And God blessed them. And God said to them, "be fruitful and multiply and fill the earth and subdue it and have dominion over the fish of the sea and over the birds of the heavens and over every living thing that moves on the earth." [29]And God said, "behold, I have given you every plant yielding seed that is on the face of all the earth, and every tree with seed in its fruit. You shall have them for food. [30]And to every beast of the earth and to every bird of the heavens and to everything that creeps on the earth, everything that has the breath of life, I have given every green plant for food." And it was so. [31]And God saw everything that he had made, and behold, it was very good. And there was evening and there was morning, the sixth day.

Genesis 1

Dare we dream of an ideal world? Could there be such a place? I'm talking about a world as it should be. A place of perfect peace, health and wholeness. A place where love reigns and violence is a foreign concept. A world where there is absolutely no cancer, no murder, no overdue bills, no shame, no hurricanes or floods. Dare we dream of a place like that? Is it silly to wonder what this kind of world would be like?

Genesis 1 shows us that it is not silly to think this way, because such a world once existed. We were engineered to live there; it's in our bones. That's why it shows up in our stories and myths and movies and imaginations and utopian visions.[1] The Bible says the memory of that perfect world is imprinted on our hearts, and no one can escape it. C.S. Lewis said it is like "remote music that we are born remembering."

The very fact that we imagine a perfect world speaks to the fact that we were made for something else. The whole human race has a deep memory of paradise lost, a faint but powerful awareness that there must be a better, different world. And we have an innate restlessness to return there, because it is the world that we were made for.

What does the Apostles' Creed mean when it confesses God as "the Maker of heaven and earth?" Genesis 1 gives us a hint, as it tells the story of God creating a good world. And in this creation account, we are confronted with his extravagant power.

---

1 Rev. Ray Cortese of Seven Rivers Presbyterian Church (FL) made this point.

THE EXTRAVAGANT POWER OF GOD

John Ortberg invites us to imagine what Genesis 1 would read like if God were less powerful, and more like us:

> In the beginning, it was nine o'clock, so God had to go to work. He filled out a requisition to separate light from darkness. He considered making stars to beautify the night, and planets to fill the skies, but thought it sounded like too much work. So he decided to knock off early and call it a day. And he looked at what he had done and he said, "it'll have to do." On the second day God separated the waters from the dry land. And he made all the dry land flat, plain, and functional, so that, behold, the whole earth looked like Idaho. He thought about making mountains and valleys and glaciers and jungles and forests, but he decided it wouldn't be worth the effort. And God looked at what he had done that day and said, "it'll have to do." And God made a pigeon to fly in the air, and a carp to swim in the waters, and a cat to creep upon dry ground. And God thought about making millions of other species of all sizes and shapes and colors, but he couldn't drum up any enthusiasm for any other animals — in fact, he wasn't too crazy about the cat. So God looked at all he had done, and God said, "it'll have to do." So he breathed a big sigh of relief and said, "thank ME, it's Friday."[2]

You cannot read Genesis and not be confronted with the extravagant power of God. God speaks, and things happen. The emptiness is filled. The darkness vanishes. The skies teem with birds, the world is green and lush. God creates humanity, and there is peace and harmony. It's really pretty amazing. Out of chaos he brings beauty and precision.

And when it's all done, after the sixth day, God says, "It is very good." Paradise. Genesis gives us the picture of a world touched in every way by the creative power of God. God looks on it and says, "Now, this is good. I love it all. I love my creation!"

John Calvin says the world that God created is "the theatre of [his] glory."[3] When you look at the world with the proper perspective, you behold God's glory. It is woven into the very fabric of things, if you have eyes to see it.

Think for a second about the size of the universe. Psalm 104:2 says that God "stretches out the heavens like a tent." This verse always makes me (Josh) think of the parachute in gym class. In my elementary school, everyone's favorite activity in gym (other than dodge ball, of course) was the parachute. Our gym teacher would bring out the chute, and we would stand around the outside and stretch it out. There was a number of games we would play, but we'd always start by lifting it up over our heads like a giant tent. Psalm 104 says that God does the same thing,

---

2 John Ortberg, *The Life You Always Wanted* (Grand Rapids, MI: Zondervan, 2002).

3 John Calvin, *Institutes of the Christian Religion* (Philadelphia, PA: Westminster, 1960 [org. 1559]), 1.5.8; 2.6.1.

but with the entire universe. He is so big that it cannot contain him. He stands outside of it as its Creator. He stretches it out like a tent.

In Isaiah 40:26, Isaiah looks up to the stars in the sky. He says, "lift up your eyes on high and see, who created these? He brings out their host by number, calling them all by name, by the greatness of his might, and because he is strong in power not one is missing." If Isaiah was stunned just looking at the night sky, what would his worship be like today if he knew that the nearest of those stars is 39 trillion miles away? And if he knew that what he was seeing in the night sky was just a tiny patch of our galaxy which has in it 100 billion stars? And that beyond our galaxy there are literally millions of galaxies? John Piper explains:

> It seems that in these days that God is enjoying keeping the astronomers on the edge of their seats with new glimpses of power. In the fall of 1989, newspapers reported the discovery by two Harvard astronomers of a "great wall" of galaxies stretching hundreds of millions of light years across the known universe. The wall is some five hundred million light years long, two hundred million light years wide and fifteen million light years thick. In case your high school astronomy has grown fuzzy, a light year is a little less than six trillion miles. The great wall consists of more than fifteen thousand galaxies, each with millions of stars.[4]

Since then, astronomers have discovered even larger clumps of galaxies that dwarf even the great wall. It's an exciting time to be an astronomer. It's an even more exciting time to be a worshipper of God. When we look at the heavens, we see the extravagant power of God.

We also see the power of God when we look at the earth. On the second day, Genesis tells us that God made the sea. Psalm 33 says that God gathers the seas in storehouses. Some translations say "jars." As big as the sea is, he gathers it into jars!

In 1521, the explorer Magellan wanted to see how deep the ocean was at a particular point.[5] He took his six longest lines and tied them together, and tied a cannonball to the end. He dropped it overboard, and ran out of line. Magellan was flabbergasted. The line was 400 fathoms (2,400 feet) long. His conclusion was that the ocean must be immeasurably deep. Based on his journals and the location people think he was in, Magellan would have needed 50 lines to hit the ocean floor. Those incredible depths speak to the extravagant power of God.

We might also talk about the heights of the mountains, the beauty of sunsets, the specificity of conditions for life to exist on earth, the wonder of our own bodies. All these things point out the extravagant power of God, the "maker of heaven and earth."

There are a couple of important implications as we think about this. First, the earliest readers of Genesis 1 lived in the time of Moses. The Hebrews had just

4 John Piper, *The Pleasures of God* (Sisters, OR: Multnomah, 1991), 93.
5 Story referenced by Andy Davis in a sermon, "Glory to God, the Creator," at First Baptist Church, Durham, NC, May 2, 2004.

been delivered out of Egypt. They were about to enter the land of Canaan, and were surrounded by nations and cultures that had their own creation stories. In most of those creation myths, the sun and the moon and sea were all understood to be gods. Instead of worshipping the One who fashioned the sun, they worshipped the sun itself. Instead of worshipping the One who created the animals, they worshipped animals.[6]

At the time it was written, Genesis 1 was a call to repentance for any who were tempted to follow the gods of the surrounding nations. It was a reminder that Yahweh, the God of Abraham, Isaac, and Jacob, was not part of the created world. He stands apart from it. He made it all!

While few people in our time are tempted to worship the sun, it is true that many take joy and pleasure and wonder and awe at the created world without even thinking to worship its Creator.

Once again, John Piper explains it this way: imagine that the person you love most in the world is called far away, for business. And let's say it's the old days — no email or Skype — so you have to wait for the postal service to deliver letters. There is nothing you like more than getting these letters. They bring you great joy and pleasure, because they are from your long lost love. Wouldn't it be foolish, then, to fall in love with the mailman? Wouldn't it be ridiculous to confuse your joy at getting the letters into thinking that the mailman was the source of the joy?

A lot of people have fallen in love with the mailman. They love creation, but never translate that into love for the Creator. Psalm 19 tells us that "the heavens declare the glory of God." The created world is a messenger telling us his wonder and power.

This isn't to say that enjoying the created world is somehow wrong. Some of us steer clear of worshipping nature, but in doing so, we neglect to delight in the created world. In Genesis 1:28-31, God blesses humanity and gives us the earth. This world is a blessing, and refusing to enjoy it is at least as grave a sin as enjoying it apart from God.

C.S. Lewis is a great example for us here. The world never got old for him. He enjoyed the things around him with a child-like wonder. Piper draws attention to this quality in Lewis:

> [Lewis] had the ability to see and feel what most of us see and do not see. He had what Alan Jacobs called "omnivorous attentiveness" (Alan Jacobs, *The Narnian*, p. xxi). I love that phrase. What this has done for me is hard to communicate. To wake up in the morning and to be aware of the firmness of the mattress, the warmth of the sun's rays, the sound of the clock ticking, the coldness of the wooden floor, the wetness of the water in the sink, the sheer *being* of things (*quiddity* as he called it). And not just to be aware but to wonder. To be amazed that the water is

---

6 Moses even uses different words than the pagan deity names for the sun and moon to make clear that these are created things.

wet. It did not have to be wet. If there were no such thing as water, and one day someone showed it to you, you would simply be astonished. He helped me become alive to life. To look at the sunrise and say with an amazed smile, "God did it again!" He helped me to see what is there in the world — things which if we didn't have them, we would pay a million dollars to have, but having them, ignore. He convicts me of my callous inability to enjoy God's daily gifts. He helps me to awaken my dazed soul so that the realities of life and of God and heaven and hell are seen and felt. I could go on about the good effect of this on preaching, and the power of communication. But it has been precious mainly just for living.[7]

Don't you want to be like that? Don't you want "omnivorous attentiveness" to everything around you? We are called to receive and enjoy the miracle of the created world as a blessing from the Maker of heaven and earth.

THE RELATIONAL CHARACTER OF GOD

When Christians confess in the Creed that God is the "Maker of heaven and earth," we are not saying that God is an impersonal First Cause, or Prime Mover (as the concept of God is sometimes called in philosophy). Genesis is saying something much greater than that. God is relational and personal; he's intimately involved in the created world.

Genesis is one of many creation stories that were circulating in the Ancient Near East. In all these other stories, humans were created as a kind of slave class. They were made to entertain the gods, or to grow food for them. It might be easy for us to poke fun at those stories, but some of us have equally unbiblical ideas about why God created the world. My wife and I (Ray) once attended a modern retelling of Milton's *Paradise Lost*. At the climax of the play, Adam asks God, "Why did you make me?" And God replies, "I was lonely."

That's *not* a biblical answer. In verse 26 of Genesis 1, God declares, "let *us* make man in *our* image, after *our* likeness." This is the earliest hint of the Trinitarian nature of God. God the Father, God the Son, God the Holy Spirit. Christianity is the only religion that teaches this. Every other theistic religion claims that God was alone in the beginning, but Christianity says that God exists in Three Persons.

This should completely change our understanding of our world. Christianity teaches that God has lived in relationship for all of eternity. He was never lonely. The Father, Son, and Holy Spirit were a perfect family, enjoying each other from all eternity past. God had perfect love within the Trinity, and yet chose to create men and women in his own image. Why? Because this is the nature of love. True love is never selfish and always wants to be shared.

---

7 John Piper, "Lessons From An Inconsolable Soul," (Desiring God Pastor's Conference, Bethlehem, PA, February 2, 2010).

You've seen this happen at the human level. A young couple gets married and has all the fun in the world. They can travel, go out to eat, enjoy time with one another — and then they go and ruin it by having kids (just kidding!). Having kids makes sense in light of the nature of relational love that God has created us with a desire for. At some point it's natural to say, "Let's extend the family. What we have with each other, let's share that love."[8]

When Christians confess God as the "maker of heaven and earth," they are also declaring that the world is inescapably relational because the Maker of the world is relational. You may think faith is primarily about rules, or traditions, or doctrines, and while those things are important and good, Genesis 1 tells us that from the beginning our faith is about relationship. At its most basic, Christianity is about a Father and his children. And when God looks at creation after humanity is made, he says "It is very good." He is like a parent standing over the crib, looking at a baby, saying, "What a miracle! I love this child so much."

Parents often make baby books for their kids in which they lovingly log their child's first steps, first words, first tooth. The kids eventually get older and can flip through these as reminders of their parents' love for them. In this way, Genesis 1 is God's baby book for all of humanity.

How do you know if you have grasped this or not? Ask yourself how you relate to other people. Do you see other people as those made in the image of God? When you look around your workplace or your neighborhood, do you see people as the objects of God's love and affection? Or are you constantly searching for faults in others, criticizing them? If you're not showing a general level of respect and care for other people, you probably haven't come to grips yet with the idea that God is the Maker of heaven and earth. You haven't connected the dots that the person you're unwilling to love is made in the image of God. This brings us to the last point.

THE REDEMPTIVE PURPOSE OF GOD

When we say that God is the "Maker of heaven and earth," we are also saying that he has a purpose for this world, and he will complete that purpose. Despite the sin and rebellion of humanity, God is committed to fulfilling his purposes for the world.

The creation story is actually a picture of salvation. Remember the place where Moses wrote all this down. The people had just been delivered from Egypt. They were wandering in the wilderness, and some actually wanted to go back to Egypt. But Moses had to continually remind them of how God delivered them in the past, and of the Promised Land he had for them in the future.

---

8 Tim Keller made this point in a sermon on Genesis 1. (Gen. 1:26-27; 2:18-25 "Made for Relationship" at Redeemer Presbyterian Church, New York, NY, October 29, 2000.)

Most commentators point out the parallels between the creation story as Moses wrote it and the story of the Exodus.[9] God brought light to the earth at creation. He brought the opposite (darkness to Egypt) in order to free the people in Moses' day. He divided the waters at creation like he divided the waters of the Red Sea in Moses' day. God caused the earth to teem with living creatures, as he would later fill Egypt with plagues of frogs, gnats, flies, and locusts. The Spirit of God hovered over the waters of creation, as he would later hover above the people in Moses' day as a cloud by day and a fire by night. Finally, both the creation story and the story of the Exodus end with Sabbath rest!

We don't want to push this comparison too far. But we do want you to see that God's creative purposes and his redemptive purposes are intertwined. To consider God's extravagant power in creation, leads us to consider his extravagant power in re-creation. Notice that John 1 begins the same way Genesis 1 does: "In the beginning..." Genesis tells us about the creation; John tells us about how God is going to go about re-creation: "The Word became flesh and dwelt among us."[10]

The Apostle Paul also uses creation language in talking about salvation. "For God, who said, 'let light shine out of darkness,' has shone in our hearts to give the light of the knowledge of the glory of God'" (II Corinthians 4:6). "Therefore, if anyone is in Christ, he is a new creation. The old has passed away; behold, the new has come" (II Corinthians 5:17).

You have an opportunity to experience the same power of God that was at work in the creation of the world. Paul says that when you trust in Jesus Christ, when you begin to trust in his death and resurrection, the God who spoke the universe into being speaks life into your heart. The God who said, "let there be light," at the beginning of time, brings resurrection light into your heart.

Some of you are languishing in darkness, even as you read this. Maybe that is why you're reading this. The gospel is inviting you to a new beginning. You can be a new creation. Embrace Jesus Christ, and he will make you new.

9 See Exodus 7-14.
10 John 1:14.

STUDY QUESTIONS:

• Why is it not only okay, but actually a necessity that we "dream of a perfect world"?

• Are you one who loves creation, but does not always connect this to greater love for the Creator?

• If God in Trinity has lived in perfect relationship for all eternity, what does that say about us, who are made in his image? What does it mean that "true love is always shared love"? Can the Christian faith ever really be lived in isolation? Do you keep people at arm's length too often?

• What do you think about the idea that Genesis 1 is "God's baby book for us"? What are the implications?

• Do you truly see all other people as those made in the image of God? Do you see people as the objects of God's love and affection? Or are you constantly searching for faults in others, criticizing others? If you are not showing a general level of respect and care for other people, how can you learn to come to grips with the idea that God is the Maker of heaven and earth?

• Many people think that Moses wrote Genesis 1. What are some of the parallels between the creation story of Genesis 1 and the exodus story (Exodus 7-14) that Moses led his people through? What do these say about the ways God's "creative" purposes and his "redemptive" purposes intertwine?

• John 1 begins with language and themes strikingly similar to Genesis 1. The God who said, "let there be light," at the beginning of time, brings resurrection light into your heart. If you feel like you are languishing in darkness right now, can you see ways that the gospel is inviting you to a new beginning?

Jesus Christ, His Only Son, Our Lord

CHAPTER 3

¹Long ago, at many times and in many ways, God spoke to our fathers by the prophets, ²but in these last days he has spoken to us by his Son, whom he appointed the heir of all things, through whom also he created the world. ³He is the radiance of the glory of God and the exact imprint of his nature, and he upholds the universe by the word of his power. After making purification for sins, he sat down at the right hand of the Majesty on high, ⁴having become as much superior to angels as the name he has inherited is more excellent than theirs.

⁵For to which of the angels did God ever say, "you are my Son, today I have begotten you"?

Or again,

"I will be to him a father, and he shall be to me a son"?

⁶And again, when he brings the firstborn into the world, he says, "let all God's angels worship him."

⁷Of the angels he says, "he makes his angels winds, and his ministers a flame of fire."

⁸But of the Son he says, "your throne, O God, is forever and ever, the scepter of uprightness is the scepter of your kingdom.

⁹You have loved righteousness and hated wickedness; therefore God, your God, has anointed you with the oil of gladness beyond your companions."

¹⁰And,

"you, Lord, laid the foundation of the earth in the beginning, and the heavens are the work of your hands;

¹¹they will perish, but you remain; they will all wear out like a garment,

¹²like a robe you will roll them up, like a garment they will be changed. But you are the same, and your years will have no end."

¹³And to which of the angels has he ever said, "sit at my right hand until I make your enemies a footstool for your feet"?

Hebrews 1:1-13

A friend burst into my (Josh's) dorm room in college, announcing that he planned to get a fish tattoo on his ankle. I was puzzled; a representation of a bass he caught on his latest fishing trip? Was this really worth memorializing on his skin? He explained that he was planning to get an *icthus* tattoo — a symbol of faith for early Christians.[1] It was an appropriate symbol for the early church because the *icthus* served as an acrostic, spelling out the center of their faith: "Jesus Christ, Son of God, Savior."[2]

The focus on Jesus is what set early Christians apart from the beliefs of the people around them. That is why the largest part of the Apostles' Creed is about Jesus. So what do Christians mean when they confess faith in "Jesus Christ, his only Son, our Lord?"

THE INEXHAUSTIBLE MYSTERY OF GOD

The Apostles' Creed is Trinitarian. It's broken into three main parts, reflecting the Bible's teaching about the nature of God. "I believe in God the Father...I believe in Jesus Christ...I believe in the Holy Spirit."

It's one thing to talk about the Trinity, but it's a whole other ballgame to try to wrap your mind around it. You might have heard some explanations like this:
- *The Trinity is like an egg*: You have the yolk, the white and the shell. But they are all one egg.
- *The Trinity is like water*: Water can be liquid, it can be ice, and it can be vapor. But all three are the same H$_2$O.
- *The Trinity is like the presidency*: Obama is president, Bush is president, Clinton is president. Different persons, but all three are president.

These all have one thing in common: they're all heresies! Hard boil an egg, peel off the shell, and what do you have? An egg! But you cannot get rid of a member of the Trinity and still have the God of the Bible. Yes, water can be liquid, ice, and steam — and I'm even told there's a triple point where water can exist in all three forms at the same time. But if you melt ice, it becomes liquid. The members of the Trinity never morph into one another. The Son never melts into the Holy Spirit. And being God is not like holding elected office. It's not as if the Father is for Social Security reform, the Son is not, and the Spirit is still polling his constituents.

It might be a little harsh to call these illustrations "heresies." The people who came up with them were no doubt well-intentioned. But in every case, the illustrations break down. The fact that people have stretched so much to come up with illustrations ought to give you a clue as to how difficult this concept is to understand.

The best illustration we can come up with is this: imagine for a second that you are a square. You're a nice little square, living on your little two-dimensional piece of paper for your whole life. You have friends: circles and triangles and

---

1   My friend also explained the versatility of the tattoo. If he were to become a missionary in a Muslim country where proselytizing was forbidden, he assured me he could have the tattoo easily modified to look like a spaceship.

2   *Iota* is the first letter in the Greek spelling of Jesus. *Chi* is the first letter for *Christos*. *Theta* for *Theou* — the possessive "God's." *Upsilon* for *huios* "Son." And *sigma* for *soter* "Savior."

lines. But then one day, someone tells you that there is something like you — and yet not like you. Something like a square — and not like a square. We call it a cube.

Imagine, being a square your whole life, and trying to wrap your mind around a cube (a figure qualitatively different than you). It would be difficult to do. Even if you could say some things about the cube, there would be still be an awful lot of mystery if you'd only lived in a two-dimensional world all your life.[3]

Similarly, there is going to be mystery when it comes to understanding the nature of God. This makes sense. In fact, the doctrine of the Trinity might be one of the best reasons to believe in the Christian God. If God does exist, wouldn't it make sense for there to be some things about him that are so different from us and our understanding that they would be hard to grasp? If you asked someone about the nature of God and they went on to describe someone who sounded an awful lot like your Uncle Al, you'd be a little suspicious. There ought to be some mystery in trying to understand a Being qualitatively different than humanity.

But does it matter if you believe in the Trinitarian nature of God? Some might be tempted to think that talk of the Trinity is fine for a theology exam, but that it makes no difference in "real" life. Why would the Creed maintain the essential nature of such a confusing doctrine?

Athanasius was bishop of Alexandria for 46 years in the 4th century. That is a pretty good run by any era's estimation: 46 years in the same job. But it was more difficult than you might imagine. During that time, Athanasius was exiled and brought back five times — all because of his uncompromising defense of the Trinity. He wrote a book on the Trinity, and his enemies kicked him out of town. He came back and wrote a worship song about the Trinity, and they kicked him out again. He clawed his way back and wrote yet another book on the Trinity — and got kicked out again.

He did this so many times they ended up naming a creed after him: the Athanasian Creed. Each time he was fired from his post, he was also threatened with death. But Athanasius knew the entire faith, the whole Christian church, would stand or fall on the doctrine of the Trinity.

Athanasius invites us to consider a practical example: the biblical teaching about prayer. The Bible says God the Father ordains all things and so we ask him for what we need. But we aren't worthy to come into his presence to ask, so Jesus brings our requests to God ("in Jesus' name we pray"). But we wouldn't even really know what to pray, if the Holy Spirit didn't come to live within us.

The Trinity is crucial to understanding prayer. Here is how Athanasius put it: take away the *Father*, and you have *no reason* to pray. Take away the *Son*, and you have *no way* to pray. Take away the *Spirit*, and you have *no desire* to pray. The

---

3 Some have pointed out that the two-dimensional/three-dimensional tension was famously developed by Edwin Abbott in his 1884 novella, *Flatland* (Oxford: Oxford University Press, 2006). While we are unfamiliar with Abbott's work, we want to acknowledge his work nevertheless.

doctrine of the Trinity is foundational, not only to our understanding of God, but to how we relate to him.

But the essential nature of the Trinity doesn't necessarily make it easy to comprehend; it is okay to admit that it is deeply mysterious. We should expect that. If you are investigating the Christian faith, don't think you have to work out every single question before you commit. It doesn't work that way. You are always going to have some unanswered questions, especially with something like the Trinity. Let us encourage you to continue to investigate, think, read, talk to Christians, and wrestle with your doubts. Don't wait until you have exhaustive knowledge of God to finally give your life to him; you will never get there.

We need to admit that we all have to live with some mystery, no matter what we choose to believe in. What we should be asking is, does Christianity help make sense of the world?

The Creed teaches us the mystery of God. But it also points to Jesus Christ, the Son of God who is Ruler and Lord over the entire world.

The Supremacy of Jesus Christ

We referenced a portion of Hebrews 1 at the beginning of this chapter. This is one of the best places to turn in order to understand the nature of Jesus Christ. From this passage we learn that Jesus is superior to the prophets, to the priests, and even to the angels.

Superior to the Prophets

Hebrews 1:1-2 reads, "long ago, at many times and in many ways, God spoke to our fathers by the prophets, but in these last days he has spoken to us by his Son, whom he appointed the heir of all things, through whom also he created the world."

In the Old Testament, a prophet was the mouthpiece of God. He spoke the very Word of God to the people of God. In many ways prophets were the greatest figures in the Old Testament. They admonished, encouraged, and made God's will known.

In many cases these prophets were celebrities, the rock stars of the covenant community. They were often dramatic in their presentation. When Elijah came through a town, every party, every dinner conversation, was about him. "What did Elijah say? Will the famine end? What's the word from the Lord? Is God pleased?"

Moses was the greatest of the prophets; he had the most to say. He alone got a glimpse of God's *shekina* glory. When he came down from the mountain, his face glowed for a month (Exodus 34:29-35).

But Hebrews 1 says that Jesus is greater than the prophets, for he hasn't just *delivered* the Word of God, he *is* the Word of God. "God has spoken to us now by his Son." He is the Word made flesh, the expressed word of our mysterious God.

When you look at the Bible, what do you look for? Information about you? Information about how to live? No doubt there is some of that in the pages of Scripture. But the Bible is not primarily about you; it's not even primarily instructions about how to live. The Bible is primarily a roadmap to Jesus.

So when the author of Hebrews says that God has now spoken to us by his Son, he's not just saying that Jesus is the best prophet, or the most recent prophet. He is saying that all the other prophets were anticipating Jesus in some way or another. Peter writes that *all* of the Old Testament prophets were looking forward to the "sufferings and glories" of Jesus Christ (I Peter 1:10-12).[4]

If he is superior to the prophets, this means Jesus is superior to all the other voices and influences in our lives. He is greater than your parents, your spouse, your education, your friend group, your favorite writer. This means we need to regularly bring all the statements and teachings that come to us from those other influences to Jesus. It doesn't mean that those other influences aren't useful, but we always need to interpret them through Jesus, not the other way around.

Superior to the Priests

Jesus is also superior to the priests. The writer of Hebrews continues: "after making purification for sins, he sat down at the right hand of the Majesty on high..." (Hebrews 1:3). Here, the writer is anticipating the argument he will make later, in chapter 4: "We have a great high priest who has gone through the heavens, Jesus, the Son of God" (Hebrews 4:14).

In ancient Israel, the role of the high priest was to represent the people in all matters before God. The high priest would bring him gifts from the people. He would offer sacrifices for their sins, and interceded on their behalf so that they could worship freely. He was something of a bridge between the people and God.

How is Jesus superior to the priests? The Bible describes him as the once-and-for-all sacrifice. His blood makes purification for sins. The Gospel writers make a big deal of the fact that, at Jesus' crucifixion, the temple curtain was torn in two. This symbolized that the way to God's presence was now open; people could come to him freely through the work of Christ.

This means the priests are out of work. The pages and pages of how and what to sacrifice — the doves, the bulls, the lambs — are swallowed up in Jesus. According to Hebrews, we no longer need the shed blood of animals to cover our sins; in Jesus, God shed his own blood for our purification. He is the one Great Sacrifice, the Passover Lamb slain for the sins of the world. God the Son does what no priest could ever do: he is the perfect sacrifice, covering all your sins, once and for all.

Do you recognize Jesus as your great High Priest? Some of us only come to Jesus as Prophet (or teacher), but never as Priest. You search the Bible for principles to live by. You do battle against the mistakes and weaknesses in your life. Jesus is your Prophet. And that's good. But you need to go to him as your Priest as well.

---

4 See also Luke 24:25-27, 44.

Following God's law is a good thing. But the fact of the matter is, we don't do it very well. And even when we seem to get it right on the outside, our motives are often impure. That is why you need Jesus as your High Priest. You can go to him and say, "You know my pain. Your blood has been shed. You know my weakness and sin. I can never try hard enough to overcome these things. Jesus, please go to the Father for me. Speak to him for me. Be my High Priest." And take comfort in this promise: "He is able to save to the uttermost those who draw near to God through him, since he always lives to make intercession for them" (Hebrews 7:25). Jesus makes intercession for you. He speaks to the Father for you.

Superior to the Angels

What image comes to mind when you think of angels? Growing up, my (Ray's) Italian Grandma Georgina had pictures of chubby, naked cherubs all over her New York City apartment. For the longest time this was my view of angels. And when you read Hebrews 1 with that idea in mind, it doesn't seem like a big deal for Jesus to be superior to them. After all, I could beat up a fat little cupid! Jesus' supremacy doesn't seem all that impressive.

But the Bible presents a very different view of angels. C.S. Lewis, in his preface to *The Screwtape Letters*, complains about the diminished view of angels that has come down to us in religious art. In Lewis' view, Medieval artists were much more faithful to the Biblical images concerning angels.

> [Italian painter] Fra Angelico's angels carry in their face...the authority
> of Heaven. Later come the chubby infantile nudes of Raphael; finally
> the soft, slim, girlish and consolatory angels of nineteenth century art,
> shapes so feminine that they avoid being voluptuous only by their total
> insipidity...[5]

Nancy Gibbs, writing about the angel craze of the late 1990s (and if you've ever been to a greeting card store, you know this is still around), observes that "for those who choke too easily on God and rules, angels are the handy compromise, all fluff, kind, non-judgmental. And they are available to everyone, like aspirin."[6]

What does the Bible tell us about angels? The word we translate as "angel" is used over 100 times in the Old Testament, and means, very simply, "messenger." Don't think of a FedEx courier with a halo. Whenever angels appear in the Bible, people have to pick themselves up off the dirt. They fall down in terror, so much so, that angels often have to begin by saying, "Fear not! Get up. You will not die." For example, the Roman centurions were frozen in fear at Jesus' tomb when an angel appeared to announce Jesus' resurrection. This happens all over the Bible.[7] When they appear, angels are always fierce and terrifying.

---

5 C.S. Lewis, *The Screwtape Letters* (San Francisco, CA: HarperCollins, 2001), 7.
6 Quoted by Alistair Begg, *What the Angels Wish They Knew* (Chicago, IL: Moody Press, 1999), 20.
7 Revelation 19:10; Daniel 10:12-13; Luke 2:10-14.

Starting with verse 5, the writer of Hebrews presents a chain of Old Testament verses that refer to the Messiah.

- Verse 5 tells us that the he would not only be a man, but the Son of God (Psalm 2:7; II Samuel 7:14).
- Verse 6 says angels will worship him (Deuteronomy 32:43; Psalm 97:7).
- Verse 7 tells us that the angels are pretty tough too, like the wind and flames of fire (Psalm 104:4). But they are primarily messengers whose job is to talk about Jesus.
- Verses 8-9 teach us about the Kingship of the Son and how he will rule (Psalm 45:6-7).
- Verses 10-12 tell us that Jesus was the Agent of the creation of the world (Psalm 102:25-27). None of the angels can say that. Jesus is God in the flesh. The Creator of the universe stepping down into his creation.
- And verse 13 speaks to his authority and power to defeat all his enemies (Psalm 110:1).

Angels are worshippers; Jesus is the object worshipped. Angels are created; Jesus is the Creator. Angels are subordinates; Jesus is the supreme King.

The Creed says, "I believe in Jesus Christ, his only Son, our *Lord*." This is the point of Hebrews 1: that you might see Jesus as Lord. The prophets were great, but Jesus is greater still. The priests ushered people into the presence of God and made purification for sins, but Jesus is greater still. The angels are fierce and powerful, but Jesus is greater still. Jesus is Lord. He is God. And Hebrews 1:3 says, "he is the radiance of the glory of God and the exact imprint of his nature."

If the Christians are right, and this is true, then when you get connected to Jesus, your status changes dramatically. In the fifth grade, I (Josh) was not cool. I had big, Coke-bottle glasses and a bowl cut, and my mom dressed me in ridiculously fluffy sweaters. But for some reason, a girl named Brandi started to like me. When that got around school, everything changed. Brandi was cool, and all of a sudden, my status in fifth grade changed dramatically. People talked to me differently. I got invited to parties, and new people sat with me at lunch.

That is a terribly superficial example. But think of how relationship can change status, even in the world of a fifth grader. Now think about what the Bible says about Jesus, how big and majestic and important he is. Let your mind rest on the Bible's promise that when you place your faith in Jesus, you are united to him. You can call him, "brother." You share in his inheritance. You are part of his body, the church.[8] It is extraordinary to think about. If you are a Christian, your status has changed because of who you are connected to.

This should not make you arrogant, but it ought to make you confident and bold and hopeful. You are connected to the King of the universe. If you believe in Jesus, you are united to the One who is supreme over all things.

But it is not just a new status. Being connected to Jesus also means you get a new mission as well. "You are not your own, for you were bought with a price" (I

---

8 Romans 8:17; Galatians 3:26-29; Ephesians 1:3-5, 11-14; I Corinthians 12:20; Romans 12:4-5.

Corinthians 6:19-20). In other words, his mission is now your mission. Paul calls us "ambassadors for Christ" (II Corinthians 5:20). What Jesus is all about, you've got to be all about.

And so you have a mission: to feed the poor and to love your neighbors; to celebrate the unique beauties of your city and to redeem its brokenness; to be pure and to fight injustice; to feast in celebration of the kingdom; to spread the good news; to use your home as a place of hospitality; to love even your enemies.

STUDY QUESTIONS:

- Some people have denied the Trinity solely because it is impossible to fully grasp. But if God does exist, doesn't it make sense that there would be some things about him that are so different that it would be hard to grasp?

- Does it matter if you believe in the Trinitarian nature of God? Why would the Creed maintain the essential nature of such a confusing doctrine? How is understanding the Trinity "foundational, not only for how we understand God, but how we relate to him"?

- Are you one who is waiting until you have exhaustive knowledge of God to finally commit yourself fully to him?

- How is Christ superior to the prophets?

- Jesus' voice is superior to any other influence in your life. What does it mean for you to bring all the statements that come from those other influences to Jesus?

- How is Christ superior to the priests? Are you one who only comes to Jesus as Prophet or teacher, but never as Priest? Why do you need him to be your High Priest?

- How does being connected to Jesus give you a new status? How does it give you a new mission?

Conceived and Born

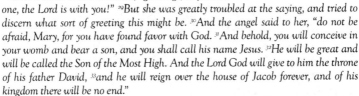

CHAPTER 4

²⁶In the sixth month the angel Gabriel was sent from God to a city of Galilee named Nazareth, ²⁷to a virgin betrothed to a man whose name was Joseph, of the house of David. And the virgin's name was Mary. ²⁸And he came to her and said, "greetings, O favored one, the Lord is with you!" ²⁹But she was greatly troubled at the saying, and tried to discern what sort of greeting this might be. ³⁰And the angel said to her, "do not be afraid, Mary, for you have found favor with God. ³¹And behold, you will conceive in your womb and bear a son, and you shall call his name Jesus. ³²He will be great and will be called the Son of the Most High. And the Lord God will give to him the throne of his father David, ³³and he will reign over the house of Jacob forever, and of his kingdom there will be no end." ³⁴And Mary said to the angel, "how will this be, since I am a virgin?" ³⁵And the angel answered her, "the Holy Spirit will come upon you, and the power of the Most High will overshadow you; therefore the child to be born will be called holy — the Son of God. ³⁶And behold, your relative Elizabeth in her old age has also conceived a son, and this is the sixth month with her who was called barren. ³⁷For nothing will be impossible with God." ³⁸And Mary said, "behold, I am the servant of the Lord; let it be to me according to your word." And the angel departed from her.

Luke 1:26-38

The Apostles' Creed declares, "I believe in Jesus Christ, his only Son our Lord, who was conceived by the Holy Spirit and born of the virgin Mary." In other words, Christians maintain that Jesus was born of a virgin. Next to the resurrection, this is the miracle that has come under the most scrutiny by skeptics.

Was Jesus really born of a virgin? Does it matter? For years, the doctrine of the virgin birth has come under attack, even by some within the church.[1] Harry Emerson Fosdick, an influential early 20ᵗʰ century pastor in New York City proclaimed, "I do not believe in the Virgin Birth and hope that none of you do." Bishop Joseph Sprague of the United Methodist Church called the virgin birth a "myth." In a letter to John Adams, Thomas Jefferson wrote, "the day will come

---

1 Mark Driscoll and Gerry Breshears, *Vintage Jesus: Timeless Answers to Timely Questions* (Wheaton, IL: Crossway Books, 2007), 89-90.

when the mystical generation of Jesus, by the Supreme Being as his Father, in the womb of a virgin, will be classified with the fable of Minerva in the brain of Jupiter."

Interestingly, Larry King, when asked if he could interview anyone from all of history, said, "Jesus Christ." "And what would you like to ask him?" King replied, "I would like to ask him if he was indeed virgin-born. The answer to that question would define history for me."

There are a lot of differing opinions as to whether Jesus was in fact born of a virgin. It's passages like Luke 1 that influenced the early church to include this doctrine in the Creed.

THE MIRACULOUS BIRTH OF JESUS

We are interested in the virgin birth, not just because it's an unusual event in history, but because it is the means of the incarnation of Jesus Christ. To incarnate means "to embody" or "to take on flesh." The Bible teaches that the great hope for the world (and for each of us) is that God has not left us alone. Though we live in a fallen world, though each of us has rebelled against God in sin and selfishness, the Bible says that God has visited the world in Jesus Christ. This is the incarnation — God has taken on flesh and walked among us. Through his physical death and resurrection, he makes it possible for ordinary people like you and me to be forgiven of our sins and live forever with God. That is good news. That's the gospel.

The Bible tells us that Jesus was born in a remarkable way — or, we should say, he was *conceived* in a remarkable way. He was born in the same manner as anyone else, but Luke tells us that Mary was a virgin when she conceived. As you know, this is not the way that babies are ordinarily made.

There are some who dismiss this story right from the start because they believe miracles cannot happen. This is a miraculous story, they reason, so the virgin birth must be a myth. Many people believe that the world can be understood empirically, which is to say using strictly observable methods. They tell us that science disproves the possibility of miracles, but this simply is not true. Scientific methodology looks only for natural causes for the things that exist around us. Thus, it does not inherently exclude the possibility of supernatural causes. Among the best scientists are many who believe not only in God, but also in miracles, including the virgin birth. One might hold the view that miracles cannot happen, but such a view is a faith-based assertion, not scientific fact. There is no way to test for the supernatural.

Further, if you allow for the possibility of God's existence, then there is nothing illogical about allowing for the possibility of miracles. As Tim Keller notes, "If [God] created everything out of nothing, it would hardly be a problem for him to rearrange parts of it when he wishes."[2]

---

2 Timothy Keller, *The Reason for God: Belief in the Age of Skepticism* (New York, NY: Dutton,

But even if miracles in general are possible, the question is whether this one in particular happened. And what does it mean if it did?

Prophesied in the Old Testament

The virgin birth of Jesus was prophesied in the Old Testament. Genesis 3:15 is what the theologians call the *protoevangelion*, or the first gospel. Speaking to the serpent, God says, "I will put enmity between you and the woman, and between your offspring and her offspring; he shall bruise your head, and you shall bruise his heel."

But then God promises that the Savior will come to rescue us. This is strange; in patriarchal societies, and throughout the Bible, children were thought of as being born from their father. Here, the Savior's father is not mentioned, implying that his father would not be of this earth.[3]

Later, God raises up a prophet named Isaiah who speaks even more clearly about the birth of the Messiah to come. "Therefore, the Lord himself will give you a sign. Behold, the virgin shall conceive and bear a son, and shall call him Immanuel" (Isaiah 7:14). Seven hundred years before Jesus' birth, Isaiah argues that people will not miss the coming of the Savior because his mother will be a virgin. Matthew quotes this verse and specifically designates it to Jesus (Matthew 1:23). He will be born of a virgin, and he shall be called Immanuel, "God with us."

Clearly Proclaimed in the New Testament

Whereas the Old Testament whispers this promise, the New Testament proclaims it loudly. It cannot be presented more clearly than in the first chapter of Luke's Gospel: Gabriel is sent "to a *virgin... and the virgin's name was Mary*" (Luke 1:27). Mary is understandably overwhelmed by this news. "And Mary said to the angel, 'How will this be, *since I am a virgin?*'" (Luke 1:34). In Greek, it literally reads, "how will this be, since I have not known a man?" The angel has to explain that this conception will be a miracle: "the Holy Spirit will come upon you and the power of the Most High will overshadow you..." (Luke 1:35). Because it is so miraculous, he adds, "for nothing will be impossible with God" (Luke 1:37).

Matthew 1 also tells this story, but from Joseph's perspective: "Now the birth of Jesus Christ took place in this way. When his mother Mary had been betrothed to Joseph, *before they came together she was found to be with child from the Holy Spirit*" (Matthew 1:18). An angel came to Joseph to persuade him not to divorce Mary. She had not been unfaithful, the angel declared, "for that which is conceived in her is from the Holy Spirit" (Matthew 1:20). Matthew reiterated the miraculous conception by adding, "[Joseph] knew her not until she had given birth to a son. And he called his name Jesus" (Matthew 1:25).

The Bible very clearly teaches that Mary was a virgin, and that Jesus was conceived solely through the miraculous power of the Holy Spirit.

2009), 86.
3   Paul employs the same language concerning "born of a woman" (Galatians 4:4).

Affirmed by the Early Church

The early Christians believed that Jesus was born of a virgin. One historian writes: "Apart from the Ebionites...and a few Gnostic sects, no body of Christians in early times is known to have existed who did not accept as part of their faith the birth of Jesus from the Virgin Mary."[4] Accordingly, both the Apostles' Creed and the Nicene Creed include a statement about Jesus being conceived by the Holy Spirit and born of the Virgin Mary.

Semper Virgo?

Finally, it is important to mention that the Bible never teaches that Mary was a virgin for her entire life. It says she was a virgin before she conceived, and all the way until Jesus was born. But it does not say she was a virgin forever.

We bring this up because by the fourth century, some arguments for the perpetual virginity of Mary became popular, and by the sixth century it was reflected in one of the church councils[5]. Some Christians[6] still teach it today. The Latin phrase is *semper virgo*, or "ever virgin." As Mark Driscoll notes, this would have made Joseph *semper bummo* — "ever bummed."[7]

Nowhere in the Bible is it said that Mary was forever a virgin. The Bible teaches that God designed sex to be a central element of marriage. Paul goes so far as to say that depriving marital intimacy is a sin (I Corinthians 7:3-5). Matthew 1:25 does say that Mary and Joseph were not intimate before Jesus was born, but notice how Matthew phrases it: "[Joseph] knew her not *until* she had given birth to a son." This clearly implies they lived as a normal married couple, physical intimacy included, after Jesus was born.

Scripture also tells us that Mary had other sons and daughters.[8] To quote Mark Driscoll and Gerry Breshears:

> In no way are we ever led to believe that Mary produced a Suburban full of kids through a succession of virgin births. Jesus' conception was unique, whereas the conception of his siblings was via the ordinary way of a husband and wife listening to old Motown baby-making music and doing what married folks are supposed to do... Much of the opposition to this simple and beautiful truth is based on the false assumption that loving, marital sexual intimacy is somehow unholy and therefore unfit for a woman like Mary.[9]

---

4 James Orr, *The Virgin Birth of Christ* (New York, NY: Charles Scribner's Sons, 1907), 138.

5 At the Second Council of Constantinople.

6 Mostly Roman Catholics; the Eastern Orthodox Church also hold to the perpetual virginity of Mary.

7 Driscoll and Breshears, *Vintage Jesus*, 94.

8 Matthew 12:46-50, 13:55-57; Mark 3:31-35; 6:3-4; Luke 8:19-21; John 2:12, 7:3-10; Acts 1:14; I Corinthians 9:5; Galatians 1:19.

9 Driscoll and Breshears, *Vintage Jesus*, 95.

When we confess the virgin conception of Jesus, we do not do so to the denigration of marital intimacy. We are instead celebrating an important fact of history that the Old Testament prophesies, the New Testament clearly proclaimed, and the early church trusted in and celebrated. But why was it important to them, and to us today?

Does it Make Any Difference?

Does this doctrine have any real importance? Rob Bell wrote a book that was popular with evangelicals a few years ago called *Velvet Elvis*. In the book, Bell suggests that belief in the virgin birth really isn't a big deal. After all, Christianity is only about how you live.

> What if tomorrow someone digs up definitive proof that Jesus had a real, earthly, biological father named Larry, and archaeologists find Larry's tomb and do DNA samples and prove beyond a shadow of a doubt that the virgin birth was really just a bit of mythologizing the Gospel writers threw in to appeal to the followers of the Mithra and Dionysian religious cults that were hugely popular at the time of Jesus, whose gods had virgin births? But what if as you study the origin of the word *virgin*, you discover that the word *virgin* in the Gospel of Matthew actually comes from the book of Isaiah, and then you find out that in the Hebrew language at that time, the word *virgin* could mean several things. And what if you discover that in the first century being "born of a virgin" also referred to a child whose mother became pregnant the first time she had intercourse?...
>
> Could a person still love God? Could you still be a Christian?
> Is the way of Jesus still the best possible way to live?
> Or does the whole thing fall apart?... [If] the whole faith falls apart when we reexamine and rethink one [doctrine], then it wasn't that strong in the first place, was it?[10]

According to Bell, the Christian faith is mainly about loving Jesus and living the way he did. Whether Jesus was born from a virgin or not doesn't affect that, so it's not crucial that a Christian believe in the virgin birth. Though Bell himself believes in the virgin conception of Jesus, he doesn't find it to be a crucial doctrine. *On that point, he is quite wrong.*

If Jesus was not born of a virgin, then the story changes significantly. Mary is a liar, inventing a story to cover up for her promiscuity. Jesus did not correct her, allowing people to go on believing this miraculous story of his birth. This makes him at least deceptive, if not an outright liar himself. It means the Old Testament texts were wrong, or at least they did not have much of anything to do with Jesus. And it makes the Gospel writers wrong in how they applied those texts to Jesus. And that makes you wonder what else they may have gotten wrong.

---

10 Rob Bell, *Velvet Elvis: Repainting the Christian Faith* (Grand Rapids, MI: Zondervan, 2005), 26-27.

It is a mistake to think you can section out one doctrine and treat it in total isolation from the rest.[11] Theology is more like an ecosystem: when a plant or animal species becomes extinct in any given ecosystem, it affects the whole of the habitat, because it is all interwoven to make the place what it is. The same is true with points of doctrine. If you remove one of the clauses of the Creed, it affects the whole story.

J. Gresham Machen wrote, "Everyone admits that the Bible represents Jesus as having being conceived by the Holy [Spirit] and born of the Virgin Mary. The only question is whether in making that representation the Bible is true or false."[12] If you think the Bible is the Word of God — God's revelation to his people — then you cannot deny the miraculous conception of Jesus. That is, not without calling into question the validity of all the other things the Bible teaches.

THE PERSON OF CHRIST

As we affirm this point, it would be easy to become so caught up in the debate on the virgin birth that we miss the larger point. The point of this doctrine is not just that God is powerful and he can do something miraculous; the point is that he came to earth, in the flesh. This is the real miracle: God came to us! Luke tells us seven things about the person of Christ in this passage.

His Name Is Jesus

"And behold, you will conceive in your womb and bear a son, and you shall call his name Jesus" (Luke 1:31). Jesus means "Savior" or "Deliverer." And that's what he came to do: to save you from your sins.

He Will Be Great

This speaks to his power and authority (Luke 1:32). John Piper explains:

A Christian who feels ashamed of Jesus Christ is like a candle feeling ashamed of the sun... Is there anything great in the world that excites you, that you go out of your way to see or hear? Christ made it! And he is ten million times greater in every respect, except sin. If you took all the greatest thinkers of every country and every century of the world and put them in a room with Jesus, they would shut their mouths and listen to the greatness of his wisdom. All the greatest generals would listen to his strategy. All the greatest musicians would listen to his music theory, and his performance on every instrument. There is nothing that Jesus cannot do a thousand times better than the person you admire

---

11 Bell did the same thing with his later book on Hell, *Love Wins* (New York, NY: HarperOne, 2011).

12 J. Gresham Machen, *The Virgin Birth of Christ* (New York: Harper & Brothers, 1930), 382.

most in any area of human endeavor under the sun. Words fail to fill the greatness of Jesus.[13]

He Is Fully Man

Jesus had a human mother. Her blood flowed through his veins in the womb. He was born. He nursed. He had his diaper changed. Mary wiped his nose and bathed him. This is part of the miracle of the incarnation. God became man. He identified with us from the womb, through birth, and through all the normal seasons of life. Jesus is fully human, so he can stand in our place, act as our substitute, and die for our sins.

He Is Fully God

In verse 32, Gabriel calls Jesus "Son of the Most High." Later in verse 35, he calls Jesus the "Son of God." These are divine titles. Jesus has the same essence, or the same "stuff," as God.

Later on, Jesus says, "I and the Father are One" (John 10:30). In the last chapter we saw that the book of Hebrews says Jesus is "the radiance of the glory of God and the exact imprint of his nature" (Hebrews 1:3). There is an abundance of texts we could quote concerning the divinity of Jesus.[14] But the point is, Jesus is God. He can truly save us because he has the authority to forgive sins, and the power to defeat death and Satan.

He Is the King

"And the Lord will give to him the throne of his father David" (Luke 1:32). David was the greatest king of Israel. In II Samuel 7, God promised that through David's line would come an even better King, one whose kingdom would have no end.

Jesus is not just the King of Israel, but the Ruler of the whole world. In fact, he is remaking the world. In Revelation he says, "I am making all things new" (Revelation 21:5). He is initiating a new kingdom, a new city, a new creation.

It is fitting that in Genesis 1, the Spirit of God hovers over the waters at the creation of the world. In Luke 1, the Spirit acts as the agent of *re-creation*, hovering over Mary so that she would conceive Jesus.

He Is Eternal

"[H]e will reign...forever, and of his kingdom there will be no end" (Luke 1:33). Jesus is eternal. He lived before he was born, and he lives beyond his resurrection and ascension. Jesus said, "I am the Alpha and the Omega, the first and the last, the beginning and the end" (Revelation 22:13). And as such, he can grant eternal life.

---

13 John Piper, "Conceived by the Holy Spirit," in Nancy Guthrie, *Come Thou Long-Expected Jesus: Experiencing the Peace and Promise of Christmas* (Wheaton, IL: Crossway, 2008), 31-32.

14 Matthew 4:7; John 1:2-3, 14; 8:12, 58; 20:28; Acts 3:15; 4:24; Colossians 1:16; Revelation 1:8, 17.

He Is Sinless

"The Holy Spirit will come upon you, and the power of the Most High will over-shadow you; *therefore* the child to be born will be called holy — the Son of God" (Luke 1:35). Did you catch the "therefore"? The uniqueness of Jesus' birth some-how connects to the fact that he is called "holy." He is set apart. He is free of the taint of human sin. And it is this uniqueness that allows him to rescue his people from their sin.

Adam had no earthly father; he was the first man. He sinned, and we all in-herited his sin nature and corruption. Jesus is the "second Adam," also without a human father. But where Adam failed, Jesus succeeded. We were condemned in Adam because of his sin, but we are redeemed in Jesus because he is holy, free of sin (Romans 5:19).

That's a lot to digest. If there is anything we can suggest in terms of applica-tion, it's worship. We should worship Jesus for all of these reasons. Jesus is the one who has come to deliver you from your sins. His great power shows that he is able to rescue you, and his humanity renders him eligible to take your place. He is the eternal King who is making a new kingdom and granting eternal life to his followers. Jesus is worthy of your worship.

Even as you are reading this, stop and worship Jesus. Praise him for who he is, and what he has done. Praise him specifically for what he has done for you. As Tim Keller so often says, "Jesus lived the life you should have lived and died the death you should have died."

THERE'S SOMETHING ABOUT MARY

We would be remiss if in commenting on the Creed, we didn't say a few more things about Mary, the mother of Jesus. While it is true that Roman Catholics seem to make too much of Mary, Protestants often do not honor her nearly enough. In fact, evangelicals rarely talk about Mary at all. How should Christians think about the mother of Jesus?

Mary is a great example for us as we attempt to love and serve God and devote our lives to him and his church. She was a recipient of grace who received love and favor from God. "Greetings, O favored one, the Lord is with you," Gabriel tells her (Luke 1:28). "Do not be afraid, Mary, for you have found favor with God" (Luke 1:30).

The word for favor is the same word for "grace." The Latin translation ren-dered this as "full of grace." Mary has been *given* grace by God. Gabriel comes to tell her that God has chosen her for something very special, but God could have chosen someone else. There were other teenage virgins in Palestine, but God chose Mary by his own initiative. She didn't do something to warrant God's blessing; he simply chose her out of his goodness.

This is a picture of how God works with us. If you are a Christian, you have been a recipient of God's grace. Like Mary, you did not deserve it, but he has still given it to you. And while Mary is not a dispenser of grace — that is the Lord's job — she is an amazing example of how we should receive it. "Behold, I am the servant of the Lord," she says. "Let it be to me according to your word" (Luke 1:38). In the face of God's favor, Mary responds with humility and trust.

Much like us, Mary probably had a plan for her life. She was excited to be engaged. She was going to marry Joseph. When Gabriel visited her, she was likely busy planning the wedding, filling out the registry, planning the big party. Then God sends an angel — and everything changes. Mary had a script for her life, but God broke in to say, "I'm writing your story in a different way."

Have you thought about how extraordinary her faith is? "Behold, I am the servant of the Lord." Some translations have it "I am the handmaiden of the Lord." In other words, "I am the lowest servant." Mary is saying, "You are God. I am not. Do with me as you wish." Do you respond that way when your plans don't work out, when God replaces your idea of what your life should look like with something else entirely?

Then Mary says, "let it be to me according to your word." She could not have known how her life would change in the coming months and years — she could not have known that people would call her a whore and a tramp,[15] that her son would be beaten and executed by the people who claimed to love him. It's likely that she only wanted to marry Joseph and live a quiet and comfortable life. In this moment, everything she thought she knew about life began to change; everything she wanted seemed to slip from her reach. And yet she responds, "let it be to me according to your word. Tell me my mission, and I will commit myself to it. I am the Lord's servant." That is amazing faith.

Mary did not lose Joseph, though she almost did. He was going to quietly divorce her, but the angel stepped in to convince him that she wasn't lying about her pregnancy. But she didn't know how Joseph would react when she responded to the angel's message. In fact, she likely expected that Joseph would leave her.

"Let it be to me according to your word." There is enough there to challenge your faith for years. When God doesn't bless your agenda, and in fact changes it completely, can you say, "I'm okay with that"? When God takes something away, or someone away, can you say "I'm okay with that"? When God takes away your respectable, carefully laid plans and sends you on a new mission, something crazy, terrifying, or unknown, can you say "I'm okay with that"?

Mary believed in the goodness of her Savior so much that she could let him rewrite the whole script. She had to sacrifice the idol of marriage, her reputation, and the possibility of a comfortable life on the altar of God's mission. "Let it be to me according to your word." By God's grace, may we pray (and live) with faith like hers.

---

15 See John 8:38-48.

STUDY QUESTIONS:

- If you grew up in the church, how did your church talk about Mary? Do you think she was over- or under-appreciated?

- Do you think Mary most likely remained a virgin after Jesus' conception? Why or why not?

- Why does it matter whether or not Jesus was born of a virgin?

- Does the teaching of Mary's virginity minimize the importance of marital intimacy?

- How is Mary's faith a special example for believers?

- What strikes you most about Mary's situation and her reaction to the angel's visit?

- Why is it a mistake to think we can section off one doctrine from all the others? How is theology like an ecosystem?

- What does it mean that Mary was "full of grace"?

- If you are a believer, what does it mean that you have received salvation by grace, and that you grow by grace?

- When God doesn't bless your agenda, and changes it completely, can you say "I'm okay with that"? When God takes away something or someone that you were counting on, can you say "I'm okay with that"?

Suffered, Crucified, Died, Buried

CHAPTER 5

[8]Finally, all of you, have unity of mind, sympathy, brotherly love, a tender heart, and a humble mind. [9]Do not repay evil for evil or reviling for reviling, but on the contrary, bless, for to this you were called, that you may obtain a blessing. [10]For "whoever desires to love life and see good days, let him keep his tongue from evil and his lips from speaking deceit; [11]let him turn away from evil and do good; let him seek peace and pursue it. [12]For the eyes of the Lord are on the righteous, and his ears are open to their prayer. But the face of the Lord is against those who do evil." [13]Now who is there to harm you if you are zealous for what is good? [14]But even if you should suffer for righteousness' sake, you will be blessed. Have no fear of them, nor be troubled, [15]but in your hearts honor Christ the Lord as holy, always being prepared to make a defense to anyone who asks you for a reason for the hope that is in you; yet do it with gentleness and respect, [16]having a good conscience, so that, when you are slandered, those who revile your good behavior in Christ may be put to shame. [17]For it is better to suffer for doing good, if that should be God's will, than for doing evil. [18]For Christ also suffered once for sins, the righteous for the unrighteous, that he might bring us to God, being put to death in the flesh but made alive in the spirit, [19]in which he went and proclaimed to the spirits in prison, [20]because they formerly did not obey, when God's patience waited in the days of Noah, while the ark was being prepared, in which a few, that is, eight persons, were brought safely through water. [21]Baptism, which corresponds to this, now saves you, not as a removal of dirt from the body but as an appeal to God for a good conscience, through the resurrection of Jesus Christ, [22]who has gone into heaven and is at the right hand of God, with angels, authorities, and powers having been subjected to him.

I Peter 3:8-22

Christianity makes a unique claim. The Head and Founder of the faith was put to death as a threat to the peace of the community in which he lived. You would think that this kind of bad press would be something to sweep under the rug. Instead, Christians put the suffering and execution of Jesus Christ at the very heart of the Apostles' Creed.

Sometimes this is called the "passion" of Jesus Christ. This comes from the Greek word *pascho*, to suffer. What does it mean to believe that Jesus "suffered, was crucified, died, and was buried"?

JESUS' PASSION WAS AN HISTORICAL EVENT

"I believe in Jesus Christ...[who] suffered under Pontius Pilate." Have you ever wondered why the Creed bothers to mention Pilate's name? It doesn't mention the main players in the Bible: not Paul, not Peter, not Moses, not Isaiah, not David. Other than Jesus and his mother Mary, Pilate is the only person named in the Creed. Why?

This was the church's way of reminding us that the Jesus we are talking about lived in real history. He was not a myth, and this is not a made-up story. If you begin a story by saying, "Ray Cannata was born when Lyndon Johnson was President," you are suggesting that this is not meant as a fairy tale.

In the Creed, we are confessing an historical event. *God is part of history.* And when he came to save us, he came in real flesh, as a real person, in real space and time. When you affirm with the Creed that Jesus "suffered under Pontius Pilate," it is a reminder that the Christian faith is not only the expression of some feeling or experience that you have had. Nor is the Christian faith a mere philosophy upon which we construct ethical principles. The Christian faith is about an *act of God in history.*[1]

This becomes immediately applicable to those of us who are discontent with the world. When you see things that are deeply broken, and are realistic enough to know they may never get fixed, God's action in history becomes important. Your only hope for the world is what is proclaimed in I Peter 3. It's not the promise of better public schools that is going to alter the course of history, nor will an economic alternative to capitalism or socialism. It's not a new streetcar in Cincinnati or better levees in New Orleans. It's not a change in health care, or voting in a new president. What *will* resolve human history is the fact that God has personally entered into our mess. He has begun and is even now working to restore the world, and will one day return to finish the job. If you are a Christian, this is your hope.

And there is something else about this action of God in history that is worth considering. *The historical nature of Jesus' passion reminds us that real people are responsible for his death.*

If you know anything about the biblical story, you will know that all sorts of people were implicated in Jesus' death.

- Pilate had a role: passing the final sentence
- The Romans were the executioners
- The religious leaders drummed up the charges

---

1   See an excellent treatment in Alister McGrath, *"I Believe": Exploring the Apostles' Creed* (Downer's Grove, IL: IVP Books, 1998), 55-57.

- The crowds chanted "Crucify him!"
- Judas betrayed him
- Peter (the author of the passage above) denied him three times

Every single person anywhere near Jesus played a role in his murder. In his preordained plan, God allowed this multiplicity of people to participate in this crime against Jesus to remind us of the contribution of all humanity. Ralph Wood writes:

> I learned an unwelcome lesson when my family and I visited Dachau, the concentration camp near Munich. With good cause the Germans have not made it an easy place to find. Having finally located the train for Dachau, we discovered that it was loaded with American college students enjoying their European spring vacation. They, too, were traveling to Dachau. It was the weekend of the NCAA basketball championship, and the train was full of raucous talk about the tournament. We might as well have been at Wendy's or McDonald's. It was not a proud moment to be an American or a Christian — traveling to a Nazi death camp as if to a sporting event.
>
> Yet something surpassingly strange happened when we Americans entered the camp gates adorned with their mocking slogan, *Arbeit Macht Frei* ("work makes free"): Silence fell over us. Everything became eerily quiet. As we walked through the dormitories and past the crematoria, no one clucked confidently about the terrible thing that the Germans had done to the Jews. We all seemed to sense, in a subterranean and unconfessed way, that *we* also could commit such unspeakable crimes. I had no desire to shout, "*they* did this," but rather, "*we* did this" — we human beings, who also killed the ultimate Jew named Jesus the Christ.[2]

The application is clear. To lay the blame for Christ's death on the Jews, or Pilate, or anyone else, is to miss the Bible's point completely. The killing of Jesus reveals the fallen nature of every person on earth.

Friends, *you* killed Jesus. Your sin did. If you really let the meaning of the Scriptures press into you, you'll notice this is not a feel-good story. One of the first things you'll see is that you're worse than you thought you were. Your sin matters. It got Jesus nailed to a tree.

Perhaps you know the hymn "Amazing Grace." One of the lines goes like this: "T'was grace that taught my heart to fear." What does John Newton mean by that? How does grace teach your heart to fear?

The grace of God shows you how deep and wicked and terrible your sin is. It also shows you the wrath of God that is poured out on sin. So when we say "Jesus Christ died for us," we ought to tremble a bit. Our sin is so offensive to God, that he killed Jesus because of it.

---

2 Ralph Wood quoted in *Exploring and Proclaiming the Apostles' Creed*, Roger E. Van Harn, *Exploring and Proclaiming the Apostles' Creed*, 113.

The next line in "Amazing Grace" is "T'was grace my fears relieved." If grace teaches your heart to fear, then how can that same grace relieve that fear? It is because both fear and relief come from the same place: the cross. Jesus' voluntary suffering tells you how much he loves you, and that he has made a way of salvation for you. "You are worse than you thought you were, but you are more loved than you ever dared to imagine."[3] This is the gospel; this is what the passion of Jesus Christ teaches us.

JESUS' PASSION IS THE WAY OF SALVATION

When we talk about the suffering and cross of Jesus Christ, we are not just embracing the *truth* of an historical event, but we're also confessing the *significance* of that event. The Creed speaks to the purpose for which Jesus died — namely, to open the way of salvation.

The theologian Alister McGrath illustrates the distinction.

> In 49 BC Julius Caesar crossed a small river with a single legion of men. The name of the river was the Rubicon, and it marked the boundary between Italy and Gaul. As an event, the crossing was not particularly interesting; the Rubicon was not a particularly wide river, and it had been crossed countless times before. But this seemingly unimportant event had a deeper meaning. The Rubicon marked a national frontier. By crossing it, Caesar declared war against Pompey and the Roman senate — with momentous results. The event was the crossing of a river; the *meaning* of that event was a declaration of war.[4]

In some ways, Jesus' death parallels the crossing of the Rubicon. He wasn't the first person to die on a cross; this was a common punishment in the Roman world. Furthermore, many people throughout history have died unjustly. Many have given their lives in exchange for others. But Peter wants us to know (and the Creed proclaims) Jesus' death was different from all the rest. Why?

The Roman Senate was not particularly interested in *how* Caesar crossed the Rubicon. And Peter (in the passage at the beginning of this chapter) is not particularly interested in *how* Jesus died. We don't get a lot of details about the death of Jesus in I Peter 3. Instead, Peter focuses on *why*. Why did Jesus die? Why did Jesus let us kill him? The key is in verse 18 — "for Christ also suffered once for sins, the righteous for the unrighteous, that he might bring us to God."

At the center of human history, a transfer took place. Theologians call this "the great exchange." Jesus was innocent, perfectly sinless, and yet God the Father treats him as if he were guilty. Do you hear it in Peter's words? "The righteous for the unrighteous." Jesus, who always obeyed his Father, who perfectly obeyed the Law, who never strayed in his relationship with God. Jesus, perfect and sinless in every way, is executed to pay for sin.

---

3 As Tim Keller, quoting the late C. John Miller, so often reminds us.
4 McGrath, *I Believe*, 61.

Peter goes on to say that this is how you get to God. In going to the Cross, he brings us to God. Jesus takes your sin upon himself, and he suffers the penalty for it. Jesus takes on our death, our curse, our condemnation, the wrath and scorn of God that should be poured out onto us. This is why he cries out "my God, my God, why have you forsaken me?" (Matthew 27:46).

Look at how the prophet Isaiah described it hundreds of years before Christ: "he was despised and rejected by men; a man of sorrows, and acquainted with grief...because he poured out his soul to death and was numbered with the transgressors; yet he bore the sin of many, and makes intercession for the transgressors" (Isaiah 53:3-6, 12).

The gospel tells us that if you are willing to turn to Jesus in faith, your sin is imputed to him. He pays for it in his own death. The righteous suffers for the unrighteous. But it's even better than that. Peter doesn't mention it here, but not only does Jesus take your sin into himself, he also gives you *his* righteousness. Theologians call this double imputation. Jesus' death does not simply get you back to zero; if that were the case, God would look at you and see someone with the potential to go either way, towards glory or judgment. The gospel says that because of what Christ has done, he sees you as completely righteous. You are clothed in the righteousness of Christ. Jesus gets your sin, and you get his righteousness. This is the "great exchange."

There should not be a single aspect of your life untouched by this. Take for example, your conscience. What do you do with your guilty conscience? If you have a pulse, you have some sense of guilt, some sense that you have not done what you should have done at some point in your life, or that you've done what you should not have.

Most people deal with this feeling in one of two ways. Some listen to that part of our culture that tells us that there is no right or wrong. We call this relativism. If you feel bad about something, obliterate those feelings by reminding yourself that there is no such thing as a morally right or wrong action. Others listen to who we might call the moralists, who tell them to make up for their failings by trying harder next time. You can work your way into alleviating your guilty conscience.[5]

If you have tried either of these approaches, you know that they don't work. Guilt has a way of coming back. You need the truth of I Peter 3. Peter says, "Jesus suffered once for all" for all your sins. You can have a clear conscience, but not because you're going to make it up to God and do better the next time. You can have a clear conscience because he paid for your sin once and for all.

Leviticus 16 describes the Day of Atonement in ancient Jewish worship. Two goats were brought out. One was killed as a sacrifice to satisfy the wrath of God for sin. But the other was set free and sent into the wilderness, carrying the sins of the people, thus symbolizing the removal of their shame and guilt.

---

5   There are an awful lot of people who end up in seminary or vocational ministry as an attempt to alleviate a guilty conscience.

Some of you are struggling with a guilty conscience even as you read this. This turns some people into hypocrites, who cope with their shame by focusing on everyone else's sin. They become fault-finders and finger-pointers. They distract themselves from their own sin by pointing out everyone else's.

Others are paralyzed by shame. We are convinced there are a lot of Christians who are not sharing their faith, or involved in mission and leadership in the church, because they are paralyzed by shame and guilt. They feel so bad about themselves that they don't believe God could ever use them. Shame takes them right out of the fight. This is how Satan works: sometimes he tempts, but even more often he accuses. Carl Trueman wrote of Martin Luther:

> It is well-known that in his writings in table conversation Luther would often refer to visits from the Devil, how the Devil would come to him and whisper in his ear, accusing him of all manner of filthy sin: "Martin, you are a liar, greedy, lecherous, a blasphemer, a hypocrite. You cannot stand before God."[6]

But Luther used the gospel to deal with these accusations. He did not deny that he was a sinner as the relativists do, nor did he promise he'd get his act together and make up for his sin, as the moralists do. Instead, Luther went to the gospel.

Luther would respond: "Well, yes, I am. And, indeed, Satan, you do not know the half of it. I have done much worse than that and if you care to give me your full list, I can no doubt add to it and help make it more complete. But you know what? My Saviour has died for all my sins—those you mention, those I could add and, indeed, those I have committed but am so wicked that I am unaware of having done so. It does not change the fact that Christ has died for all of them; his blood is sufficient; and on the Day of Judgment I shall be exonerated because he has taken all my sins on himself and clothed me in his own perfect righteousness."[7]

Charles Spurgeon said it this way:

> My hope lives not because I am not a sinner, but because I am a sinner for whom Christ died; my trust is not that I am holy, but that being unholy, he is my righteousness. My faith rests not upon what I am, or shall be, or feel, or know, but in what Christ is, in what he has done, and in what he is now doing for me. On the lion of justice the fair maid of hope rides like a queen.[8]

Use the gospel to battle your guilt. This is one of the reasons to regularly celebrate the Lord's Supper in worship. Communion is an opportunity to remind ourselves that he makes us clean. His body broken. His blood poured out. All so that our sin could be dealt with. And as we take in these elements, we are

---

6 Carl Trueman, "Thank God for Bandit Country," *Reformation 21*, June 2009.

7 Ibid.

8 Charles H. Spurgeon, ed. Alistair Begg, *Morning and Evening: A New Edition of the Classic Devotional Based on the Holy Bible* (Wheaton, IL: Crossway, 2003), 550.

reminded that Christ lives in us, and that when God looks at us, he sees the righteousness of Christ.

The suffering, death, and burial of Christ — historical events in which we all participate — is the way of salvation for those who trust in Christ. But these events also teach us about the nature of the Christian life, that we may know what it means to follow the path of our Savior.

Jesus' Passion Shows the Nature of the Christian Life

The Cross should shape our lives. One author calls this "cruciformity."[9] We are told to follow Jesus, to take up our cross, to live as he lived. But what does this cruciformity look like?

Identify with Jesus

Peter talks about baptism in verse 21. It seems a little out of place at first glance, but baptism marks us off as belonging to Jesus, as well as to his people. It is a sign and a seal of the covenant of grace. It is like a wedding ring; rings don't make you married, but they do show you that you are.

That is why Peter writes in verse 21, "Baptism now saves you." It saves you not by outward water as if by magic. It "saves you" because it is the initiation rite into the one place of safety in a world flooded with death: faith in Christ.

Peter brings it up right after talking about Noah. Noah and his family are saved as they get into the ark. The waters flood the world and everyone dies, but they are saved because they are in the boat. It is fitting, then, that one of the earliest Christian symbols for the church was an ark. When you are baptized, it is a picture of being included in the covenant community, the church, the only safe place in a world flooded with death. By his passion, Christ opens the way to becoming eternally identified with him.

Identify with His Suffering

Those in Christ identify with Jesus, but more specifically, we identify with his suffering. Peter spends an awful lot of time talking about suffering in this letter. In I Peter 3:8-17, he stresses that when Christians suffer for the sake of Jesus, they should not be surprised. For many Christians in the early church this suffering meant physical persecution and death. For others it took the form of the "reviling and slander" that Peter mentions.

Let us give you an example. In Peter's day, every craftsman belonged to a guild in order to do business. These guilds were like modern unions, but even more important. Each local chapter of the guild was devoted to a pagan god, and every member was required to go to the temple and make sacrifices to that god. When

---

9 Michael J. Gorman, *Cruciformity* (Grand Rapids, MI: Wm. B. Eerdmans, 2001).

someone came to Jesus and joined the church, they'd know that they were only to worship the Triune God, and would refuse to take part in the pagan temple sacrifices. For this they would be kicked out of the guild. They were blacklisted in their trade, cut off from their means of making a living. This is one reason Christians in the book of Acts began to live sacrificially, taking care of one another.

Still today, identifying with Jesus will cost you something. What is it costing you? In Sudan, Indonesia, Afghanistan, and Iran, Christians are being tortured and killed on a daily basis. I hope none of you reading this have to experience anything like that. Just knowing this happens ought to drive us to our knees to pray for our brothers and sisters who are persecuted for their faith.

Even in the United States, identifying with Christ will cost you. It will cost you money as you give generously to bless other people, or pass over a higher-paying job so you can stay in the community where your church worships. It might cost you a promotion as you refuse to step over other people to climb the ladder, or refuse to put in 80 hours at the office so that you can instead spend more of your time with family and friends, or serving your neighbors. It's going to cost you heartache as you involve yourselves in the messiness of other people's lives and share their burdens. It will cost you time as you open your house to show hospitality to your neighbors. It might cost you a girlfriend or boyfriend who you know is not helping you follow Christ. It might cost you some security as you choose to move toward pain, perhaps by moving into a hurting neighborhood in your city.

We don't know how God is calling you but we can say without a shadow of a doubt that following his call will cost you. And if it hasn't cost you anything yet, you might ask if you're really following Jesus faithfully. Peter is clear: identifying with Jesus through this great exchange always involves identifying with his suffering.

Identify with Christ's Victory

Fortunately, Peter doesn't conclude the passage by saying, "Guys, I wish I didn't have to tell you all this stuff about suffering, but it's true. So suck it up, and bear it." That's *not* what he says, and it's not what the Apostles' Creed has in mind.

The Christian story is ultimately hopeful. Suffering, though real, is not the end of the story. If you identify with Christ in his suffering, you also get to identify with him in his *victory*. I Peter 3:21 reminds us that Jesus did not suffer and stay in the grave. He rose again, and is the firstborn of many others. You, too, will rise if you are in Christ.

Peter goes on to say that Jesus "has gone into heaven and is at the right hand of God, with angels, authorities, and powers having been subjected to him" (I Peter 3:22). Christ has risen and ascended into heaven, where he rules as King. And all those in his Kingdom, being united to him in suffering, will be united with him in glory.

When you trust in that, it changes everything.

STUDY QUESTIONS:

- Why do you think the Creed mentions Pontius Pilate?

- How does knowing that the passion of Christ was a real event in history bring comfort and hope to your struggles today?

- Why does the old hymn "Amazing Grace" say that grace causes our hearts to fear? Why does is it say that the same grace relieves those same fears? Does the cross make you tremble? Is the cross a comfort for you? How?

- Why do you think Peter is more concerned here about the "why" than the "how" of the passion?

- What is the "great exchange"? How does it help you deal with your guilt? Fears? Your sense of purpose? Past experiences of abuse? Depressive feelings? Your mission to others?

- How is communion a means of grace in your life? How is it used to battle guilt or fear or depression in your life?

- How can you identify with Jesus' sufferings more fully? How does this shape your mission? How can this impact your decisions about how to serve in church? Or where to live?

- How can you identify more fully with Jesus' victory? How does this shape your mission? The way you view and serve your neighbors?

He Rose Again From the Dead

CHAPTER 6

¹³That very day two of them were going to a village named Emmaus, about seven miles from Jerusalem, ¹⁴and they were talking with each other about all these things that had happened. ¹⁵While they were talking and discussing together, Jesus himself drew near and went with them. ¹⁶But their eyes were kept from recognizing him. ¹⁷And he said to them, "what is this conversation that you are holding with each other as you walk?" And they stood still, looking sad. ¹⁸Then one of them, named Cleopas, answered him, "are you the only visitor to Jerusalem who does not know the things that have happened there in these days?" ¹⁹And he said to them, "what things?" And they said to him, "concerning Jesus of Nazareth, a man who was a prophet mighty in deed and word before God and all the people, ²⁰and how our chief priests and rulers delivered him up to be condemned to death, and crucified him. ²¹But we had hoped that he was the one to redeem Israel. Yes, and besides all this, it is now the third day since these things happened. ²²Moreover, some women of our company amazed us. They were at the tomb early in the morning, ²³and when they did not find his body, they came back saying that they had even seen a vision of angels, who said that he was alive. ²⁴Some of those who were with us went to the tomb and found it just as the women had said, but him they did not see." ²⁵And he said to them, "O foolish ones, and slow of heart to believe all that the prophets have spoken! ²⁶Was it not necessary that the Christ should suffer these things and enter into his glory?" ²⁷And beginning with Moses and all the Prophets, he interpreted to them in all the Scriptures the things concerning himself. ²⁸So they drew near to the village to which they were going. He acted as if he were going farther, ²⁹but they urged him strongly, saying, "stay with us, for it is toward evening and the day is now far spent." So he went in to stay with them. ³⁰When he was at table with them, he took the bread and blessed and broke it and gave it to them. ³¹And their eyes were opened, and they recognized him. And he vanished from their sight. ³²They said to each other, "did not our hearts burn within us while he talked to us on the road, while he opened to us the Scriptures?" ³³And they rose that same hour and returned to Jerusalem. And they found the eleven and those who were with them gathered together, ³⁴saying, "the Lord has risen indeed, and has appeared to Simon!" ³⁵Then they told what had happened on the road, and how he was known to them in the breaking of the bread.

Luke 24:13-35

he Apostles' Creed does not let us stop with the suffering and death of Jesus Christ. Instead, it pushes us forward to the message of Easter: his resurrection. The Creed proclaims that "on the third day he rose again from the dead." This is the most astounding claim in all human history. Jesus Christ truly died, and truly went to the grave. But he did not stay there.

What does it mean for Christians to believe in Easter? My (Ray's) wife asked my daughter Rachel that question one year. She said, "the bunny!" My wife reminded her that it also reminds us that Jesus rose from the dead, to which Rachel replied, "Yes! And the Easter Bunny gave him candy!" It's safe to say we still had some work to do.

Jesus' victory on Easter is certainly cause for celebration — in fact, it should be the root of all of our celebration. But in order to talk about Christ's defeat of death, we have to begin by admitting that death terrifies us.

An Aversion to Death

All of us are afraid of death, some of us more than others. My (Josh's) dad grew up in Boston. His favorite baseball player was Ted Williams — the greatest hitter of all time. He was the last person to hit over .400 in a season.[1]

When Ted Williams died, a fight broke out among his children. His daughter wanted to have her father cremated and his ashes scattered off the Florida coast. But the son and the other daughter wanted to put dad on ice — literally. Shortly after his death, they rushed him to a cryogenic lab in Scottsdale, Arizona, and had him frozen. He remains there today (some say suspended upside down, others say in two pieces) in a tomb of liquid nitrogen frozen at -350°.[2] Why would the Williams family go to such lengths to try to overcome death?

Our fear of death is not without reason. The Bible teaches that death is a product of the fall of humanity. Genesis 3 explains that Adam and Eve, the first family, sinned against God, not only allowing evil into the world, but granting death its power, too. Death is not natural; it's not part of the good plan of God for humanity. We were not built to die.

Most fear death for other reasons as well. Death is the end of everything we know. There is nothing more abrupt, nothing more permanent, nothing more frightening. For many, the uncertainty of what comes next keeps us petrified.

Despite our violent movies and video games, our culture is terrified of death. We can deal with it in fantasy, but it's the last thing we want to enter into the conversations of real life. J.I. Packer says death is the "new obscenity, the nasty thing that no polite person nowadays will talk about in public."[3] Think of all the euphemisms we come up with so we won't have to even say the word: "passed

---

1   And that was all the way back in 1941, when he hit .406.

2   This sounds like the opening sequence to an episode of a science-fiction TV show. Sometimes truth is stranger than fiction.

3   J.I. Packer, *Affirming the Apostles' Creed* (Wheaton, IL: Crossway, 2008), 85.

away," "expired," "departed," "breathed one's last," "gone to his rest." (We found a web page listing 216 of these.) Our personal favorite was a clinical one: "*negative patient care outcome.*" Apparently, we can't even bear to say the words "she died."[4]

Given the human aversion to death, it's no wonder that Cleopas and his friend in Luke 24 are so despondent. And it wasn't just them; everyone who was close to Jesus was downcast. Most could not stand to be anywhere near the cross. Other than a few women, none even ventured a visit to the tomb. They were crushed, not only because their friend had died, but because he had taken their hopes and dreams with them. The one they believed to be the Son of God and King of kings had been brutally murdered. How could this have happened? By all appearances, it was a cruel twist of fate. They had left jobs and homes to follow Jesus, and now he was gone. So they found themselves questioning, wondering and afraid. "We had hoped he was the one to redeem Israel" (Luke 24:21). But Jesus was dead, so this could not be true. He couldn't possibly be the Redeemer of Israel.

"HE DESCENDED INTO HELL"

We need to pause here for a moment. We've been talking about this from the side of the living — our aversion to death as well as Cleopas and his friends' sorrow at Jesus' death. But we might stop to ask, what was Jesus doing in the time between his death on Friday and his resurrection on Sunday? Where was he and what was he doing?

You will notice that between stating that Jesus was "crucified, died, and was buried," and that "he rose again," the Creed says that Jesus "descended into hell." Or, we should say, some translations of the Creed say that. For clarity's sake, many churches and denominations have decided to translate it, "He descended to the dead." We should consider the meaning of this statement.

The early church took its first stab at the Creed around AD 200. The intention was to summarize the teachings of the Bible for the purpose of instructing new converts, to guard all believers against heresy, and to unite Christians on the core elements of the faith.[5] The Creed went through several revisions, and the phrase "he descended into hell" did not appear until AD 390.[6]

What was the church trying to say by adding this in? Or, to put it another way, what biblical truth was the church trying to affirm? There are three main interpretations of this phrase.

First, some argue that the phrase "he descended into hell" is trying to communicate that Jesus took the full brunt of God's wrath on the cross. In this view, the Creed is affirming again that Jesus fully paid for your sins. He did not only

4   This is also why most people no longer have funeral services in homes or churches, but in funeral homes. These days we bury our loved ones' bodies in pleasant cemeteries outside town, rather than in the churchyard (or our own backyard!).

5   See chapter 1 for a fuller discussion of the purpose and usefulness of the Creed.

6   Wayne Grudem, *Systematic Theology: An Introduction to Biblical Doctrine* (Grand Rapids, MI: Zondervan, 1994), 586.

suffer physically, he suffered spiritually. This is why he cries out on the cross, "my God, my God, why have you forsaken me?" (Matthew 27:46). It is not just physical death Jesus is experiencing, but the wrath of God against sin. This was John Calvin's view,[7] and that of several others.[8]

This is absolutely true. Jesus did bear the brunt of God's wrath for the sins of the world on the cross, so you can accurately say that on the cross Jesus experienced hell. But we don't think this is what the early church meant when they put this phrase in the Creed. For one thing, if this is what the Creed's authors intended, they have placed the phrase in the wrong spot! It should say something like "he suffered under Pontius Pilate, was crucified, went to hell, and then died and was buried." But that's not what the Creed says. Rather, it says that he suffered, died, and was buried, and *then* descended to hell. The phrase's placement in the Creed makes this interpretation unlikely.

A second view says that Jesus actually went to hell after dying on the cross. Jesus doesn't just suffer hell on the cross, but he actually goes down to hell and spends three days there. This has some theological merit. In this view Jesus receives the full justice in our place as the one judged.

But there is a major problem with this view: you cannot find it in the Bible. Every other doctrine of the Apostles' Creed is easily located in the biblical text, but this idea simply isn't there. And the proof texts some have offered are frankly not very convincing.[9]

What's more, there are biblical texts that seem to contradict this understanding. Jesus says to the thief on the cross: "*Today* you will be with me in Paradise" (Luke 23:43, emphasis added). When his suffering on the cross is nearing its end, Jesus cries, "It is finished" (John 19:30), strongly suggesting that his work of paying for sins is complete. There should be no punishment left for Jesus to endure at this point. Shortly after, Jesus says, "Father, into your hands I commit my spirit" (Luke 23:46). Again, this implies that he is going immediately to be with his heavenly Father.

So if the point of the Apostles' Creed is to summarize things the Bible clearly teaches, this cannot be the correct interpretation.

The third view says that this phrase in the Creed is another way of affirming that Jesus actually died. This mainly arises from a translation issue. The Greek word used in the Apostles' Creed is *hades*, which sometimes gets translated as "hell." *Hades*, like the Hebrew word *sheol*, means "the grave, the place of the dead." It is a fairly general term. The term *gehenna*, which is also used in the New Testament, means "the place of punishment" and is what we normally mean when we say "hell." But the Creed *does not* say, "Jesus descended into *gehenna* [hell]." It says, "he descended into *hades* [the grave, or the place of the dead]."

---

7 John Calvin, *Institutes of the Christian Religion*, 2.16.10.

8 See also the Heidelberg Catechism, Question 44.

9 For example, see Acts 2:27, Romans 10:6-7, Ephesians 4:8-9, I Peter 3:18-20, I Peter 4:6. For a discussion of these passages, see Grudem, 586-593.

This matches what we see in the Bible — a constant emphasis on the fact that Jesus really died. He didn't swoon, faint, or pass out. When he rose from the dead, he truly rose from the dead. He was not merely resuscitated.

This understanding matches what we see historically in the battles the early church had to fight. In the first few centuries, the church regularly had to answer those who denied the full humanity of Jesus. There were some who thought that Jesus was so holy and divine that he could feel no pain and experience no death.[10] But the Creed states loudly and clearly (and even repetitively) that Jesus was human in every way, except that he did not sin. His death, therefore, is a real death.

The *Westminster Larger Catechism* confirms this view. Question 50 asks, "wherein consisted Christ's humiliation after his death?" The answer: "Christ's humiliation after his death consisted in his being buried, and *continuing in the state of the dead, and under the power of death* till the third day, which hath been otherwise expressed in these words, 'He descended into hell'" (emphasis added).

This was likely the intention of the early church.[11] It affirms something the Bible clearly teaches and states something that all Christians should affirm. But it can also be a source of great hope to you.

We've been talking a lot of doctrine in this chapter, but we hope you see the practical significance of these ideas. The mortality rate of everyone reading this book will be 100%. We will all die; the good news is that Jesus has been there before us. And if you are united to him, he will see you through to the other side.

In one of his hymns, Richard Baxter writes, "Christ leads me through no darker rooms / Than he went through before." Jesus tasted death (Hebrews 2:9) and has gone through exactly what you will go through, preparing and sanctifying the way. Thus, you can follow him with confidence.

Theologian Wayne Grudem puts it this way:

> Christ in his death experienced the same things believers in this present age experience when they die: his body remained on earth and was buried (as ours will be), but his spirit (or soul) passed immediately into the presence of God in heaven (just as ours will). Then on the first Easter morning, Christ's spirit was reunited with his body and he was raised from the dead — just as Christians who have died will (when Christ returns) be reunited to their bodies and raised in their perfect resurrection bodies to new life.[12]

An Apparent Foolishness

Let's turn our thoughts now from the death of Jesus to the resurrection. When Christians say Jesus rose from the dead, they are claiming something that is

---

10 Barclay, *The Apostles' Creed*, p. 104.

11 In defense of this being the meaning intended by the early church, note that Rufinus (340-410) wrote in his commentary on the Creed that the Latin church was not erroneous in leaving out this phrase, as it was meant to communicate the same thing as "dead and buried."

12 Grudem, *Systematic Theology*, 593.

apparently absurd. Those who have been followers of Christ for a long time are at a distinct disadvantage here. You may forget how shocking this really is. The Easter story is the most bizarre and apparently foolish thing ever taught.

It is so strange, in fact, that many work very hard to explain away the resurrection, or reinterpret the events. For example, there are some (even some within the church) who say that Jesus rose again, but not in a bodily sense. Yes, they say, Jesus is alive, but only through his legacy. We keep his memory alive by living out his values.

I (Josh) remember first encountering this idea while taking a religion class in college. We studied a 20th century theologian named Rudolph Bultmann who claimed the experience of the resurrection of Jesus was central to the Christian message, but that in an age of electric lights and radios, no one could possibly believe in a physical resurrection.[13] You will hear people say things like this from time to time: "I believe in the resurrection of Jesus," they might say. "I just don't believe in an empty tomb."

This would have been utterly incomprehensible to Jesus' disciples. The early disciples did not announce that they were going to keep Jesus' memory alive; they said that *he really was alive*. Remember, they weren't just risking their reputations by presenting a paper at an academic conference; they were risking their own lives to proclaim the resurrection. Many of them lost their lives doing just that.

It's tempting to think that ancient people believed more naturally in miracles than we moderns, but the idea of a resurrection in the ancient world was just as unbelievable then as it is now. Jesus told his disciples several times that he would die and rise again on the third day. But in Luke 24, no one seems to have been expecting this. No one was walking around thinking, "It's the third day, I sure can't wait for Jesus to rise from the dead!" No one thought this way. Where were all the disciples on Sunday morning? They were all in hiding. And the female followers went to the tomb, but why did they go? They brought spices and perfume to embalm the body. Nobody was expecting a resurrection.

And why not? Because it was just as unbelievable then as it is now. Perhaps for different reasons, but resurrection didn't fit the worldview of the first century any more than it fits that of the 21st. For Greeks, salvation was a liberation of the soul from the body. The idea of a physical, bodily resurrection was ludicrous to the Greco-Roman mind. Aeschylus, the Greek playwright, wrote, "Once a man has died, and the dust has soaked up his blood, there is no resurrection."[14] The Greeks certainly weren't expecting resurrection, which is why Paul maintains the gospel message is "foolishness to the Greeks" (I Corinthians 1:23).

But what about the Hebrews? Some Jews believed there would be a future resurrection, but this was thought to be a corporate event at the end of time, when

---

13 Bultmann quoted in Alister E. McGrath, *Christian Theology: An Introduction* (New York, NY: Wiley-Blackwell, 2001), 400.

14 Quoted in N.T. Wright, *The Resurrection of the Son of God* (Minneapolis, MN: Fortress Press, 2003), 32.

the whole world was renewed. First-century Hebrews did not have a concept of individual resurrection.

It wasn't any easier for first-century people, Jew or Greek, to believe. But many did.

A PUBLIC TRUTH

There are three things that led early Christians to argue for the bodily resurrection of Jesus.

Eyewitnesses

First, there were eyewitnesses who saw the resurrected Christ. We might call this *empirical evidence*. Cleopas and his friend (Luke 24), Peter and the other disciples (John 20), the women at the tomb (Luke 24:10) — all had encounters with Christ in the days after his death. Paul even says there were over 500 that saw the resurrected Jesus at the same time (I Corinthians 15:6).

When the New Testament was being written, most of the witnesses listed by Paul and the evangelists were still alive. It's as if they're saying, "If you don't believe me, go ask them." This is how one did footnotes in the ancient world.

If there weren't eyewitnesses of the resurrected Jesus, then Christianity could never have gotten off the ground. Remember, the story was just as weird then as it is now. If you were a skeptic and Luke or Paul or Peter or Matthew or John told you about the resurrection, and offered as proof the testimony of others who had also seen the resurrected Christ, what would you do? You would likely go and talk to them. People in the ancient world weren't stupid. C.S. Lewis calls it "chronological snobbery" when we just assume everyone in former times were more ignorant or uneducated than we are today. The consistent testimony of eyewitnesses to the resurrected Jesus allowed Christianity to get off the ground in the very backyard of the empty tomb.

Explosive Growth

Second, only the resurrection can account for the explosive growth of the early church. Had the resurrection not occurred, there is no chance a tiny band of Jesus followers could have multiplied to several thousand people by AD 40 and to 34 million people by AD 350 (more than half the Roman Empire's population).

Think of it this way: if the tomb wasn't empty, and Jesus' body was still there, the opponents of the early church could simply have produced the body, and Christianity would have been crushed. They could have just pulled out the corpse and said, "See! These Christians are nuts!" Everyone would have gone home. But this is not what happened. The tomb was empty.

I (Josh) had my own crisis of faith in grad school, when I was regularly reading skeptics like Marx, Freud, Durkheim, and Feuerbach. I remember sitting in Buzz Coffeeshop in Oxford, Ohio, wondering if I could really believe that Jesus had risen from the dead. I wrote in my journal, "either Jesus really rose from the dead, or this is the weirdest, most unlikely thing that ever happened in human history — that people on large scale would believe this, have their lives changed by this, even die for it."

When faced with the circumstances, these are the only logical conclusions — either Jesus really did rise from the dead, or the growth of the church is the strangest phenomenon in the history of the world. As hard as it is to believe in the resurrection, I concluded that it would be much harder to believe in any of the alternatives.

N.T. Wright (who has done some of the finest scholarship on the resurrection) explains:

> The lines of historical enquiry point relentlessly inward to the first day of the week after Jesus' crucifixion. Once you allow that something remarkable happened to his body that morning, all the other data fall into place with astonishing ease. Once you insist that nothing so outlandish happened, you are driven to ever more complex and fantastic hypotheses to explain [away] the data. For the historian...the answer should be clear.[15]

There is one other piece of evidence for the resurrection: the testimony of Scripture. In Luke 24:24-27, Jesus tells the men that they should not have been surprised by the reports from the women that the tomb was empty; they should have been expecting it all along. "You are slow to believe all that the prophets have told you," he tells them. I think we would all have liked to have been there for this Old Testament seminar that Jesus does with these disciples. He must have talked to them about the story of the creation and fall, the promises to Abraham, the exodus from Egypt, the law, the kingdom, the exile, the psalms, the prophets — and in each spot, Jesus would have shown them that they had every reason to expect the resurrection.

Jewish tradition was right. There would be a collective, corporate resurrection of the dead. What they missed was that the resurrection had already begun. It began with Jesus, the Messiah!

Maybe you think it would be easier to believe in the resurrection if Jesus appeared to you. I don't think we can dispute that it would certainly make the story easier to believe if we were able to encounter the risen Christ the same way the apostles did. But we do have the Scriptures, the same evidence that Jesus gives to the men on the Emmaus Road; if Jesus himself used it to convince others of his resurrection, surely he can convince us.

When Jesus taught them from the Bible, their "hearts burned within them" (Luke 24:32). Jesus explained from the Old Testament how he was the Messiah, the fulfillment of all their hopes and the end of all their fears. It meant a whole new age had dawned! Sins could be forgiven and a new world was being ushered

---

15 N.T. Wright and Marcus Borg, *The Meaning of Jesus: Two Visions* (San Francisco, CA: HarperOne, 2007), 124.

in. The resurrection of Jesus pledges that the resurrection of all believers is on its way.

Does your heart burn as you think about this? Have you recognized how it all fits together? Have you realized that this is the best news on earth? Are you exhilarated at the thought that Christ has risen, that we need not fear death? Death *is* terrible. It is wicked and awful, and powerful enough to consume us. But the resurrection is even greater.

Consider how the third-century bishop Cyprian counseled others after the death of a loved one:

> [O]ur brethren who have been freed from the world by the summons of the Lord should not be mourned, since we know that they are not lost but sent before; that in departing they lead the way; that as travelers, as voyagers are wont to be, they should be longed for, not lamented... and that no occasion should be given to pagans to censure us... on the ground that we grieve for those who we say are living.[16]

What do you do in the face of death? How do you handle the thought of your own death? If you had the money, would you be signing up for cryogenics? Cyprian tells us to have a party! Christ is risen and in the end, this is all that matters. This is what the Easter message is about.

> Soar we now where Christ has led, Alleluia!
> Following our exalted head; Alleluia!
> Made like him, like him we rise: Alleluia!
> Ours the cross, the grave, the skies, Alleluia![17]

---

16 Quoted in Rodney Stark, *The Rise of Christianity: A Sociologist Reconsiders History* (Princeton, NJ: Princeton University Press, 1996), 81.

17 Charles Wesley, "Christ the Lord is Risen Today."

STUDY QUESTIONS:

- How is Easter celebrated in your home? Among your friends? At your church?

- Do you often think or dream about dying?

- Is it possible to believe in the resurrection in our generation?

- Other religious movements have thrived following the death of a prophet who said he brought some new message from God. How could the church have grown so explosively in the same land where Jesus was killed if he had not miraculously risen as they claimed he had?

- Does your "heart burn within you" as you think on the resurrection of Jesus?

- How does the resurrection change how we view death? Bishop Cyprian (AD 251) says it is cause for celebration. What do you think?

- Are there people in your life now facing loss who can be comforted by your witness to the resurrection? How might the resurrection affect the way you minister to them in word and in deed? How can you be faithfully present to them today?

He Ascended Into Heaven

CHAPTER 7

*¹In the first book, O Theophilus, I
have dealt with all that Jesus began
to do and teach, ²until the day when
he was taken up, after he had given
commands through the Holy Spirit
to the apostles whom he had chosen. ³He
presented himself alive to them after his suffering by
many proofs, appearing to them during forty days and speaking about the kingdom
of God.*

*⁴And while staying with them he ordered them not to depart from Jerusalem, but
to wait for the promise of the Father, which, he said, "you heard from me; ⁵for John
baptized with water, but you will be baptized with the Holy Spirit not many days from
now."*

*⁶So when they had come together, they asked him, "Lord, will you at this time restore
the kingdom to Israel?" ⁷He said to them, "it is not for you to know times or seasons
that the Father has fixed by his own authority. ⁸But you will receive power when the
Holy Spirit has come upon you, and you will be my witnesses in Jerusalem and in all
Judea and Samaria, and to the end of the earth." ⁹And when he had said these things,
as they were looking on, he was lifted up, and a cloud took him out of their sight. ¹⁰And
while they were gazing into heaven as he went, behold, two men stood by them in white
robes, ¹¹and said, "men of Galilee, why do you stand looking into heaven? This Jesus,
who was taken up from you into heaven, will come in the same way as you saw him
go into heaven."*

Acts 1:1-11

The book of Acts was written by a first-century evangelist and pastor named Luke, who was a traveling companion of the apostle Paul. Luke's first book was an account of the life of Christ commissioned by a wealthy man named Theophilus. Acts is the companion volume, not about the life of Christ, but about Christ's work in and through his church.

Acts opens with an account of the ascension of Jesus. You might tend to think that this should have gone at the end of Luke, wrapping up the earthly ministry of Jesus. But it fits even better at the start of Acts, as the Creed's assertion that Jesus "ascended into heaven and is seated at the right hand of the Father Almighty" is what gave the church both confidence and purpose in their mission. When Christians confess that Jesus "ascended into heaven," we confess his exaltation.

THE EXALTATION OF JESUS

The Christian faith leaves footprints wherever it goes. One of the most highly "trafficked" areas is the literature of the western world. In an article called "The Christian Novelty," Peter Leithart makes this very point. He notes a significant shift in the literature of western civilization before and after Jesus.

Ancient literature before Jesus is mainly *tragedy*. The stories always end badly for the major players, which reflect the dominant worldview of that culture. But after Jesus, things change. There is a shift from *tragedy* to *comedy*, where stories most often end happily for the main characters. Leithart says: "at the end of a tragedy everyone is dead. At the end of a comedy, everyone is married."[1]

William Butler Yeats notes that tragedy is at the heart of classical civilization, comedy at the heart of the Christian one.[2] W.H. Auden observes that even Greek comedies retained a strong element of tragedy. Leithart elaborates: "in classical comedy the characters are exposed and punished: when the curtain falls, the audience is laughing and those on stage are in tears. In Christian comedy the characters are exposed and forgiven: when the curtain falls, the audience and the characters are laughing together."[3]

But why is this true? The only thing that can explain this colossal shift in culture is the resurrection of Jesus. Western civilization learned to laugh in the face of death because Jesus was victorious over death. Both the audience and the characters are able to laugh when the curtain falls because Jesus walked out of the tomb and ascended into heaven, assuming his rightful place as King — a happy ending.[4] This is why Christians celebrate the ascension.

It was not enough that Jesus rose again from the dead. By itself, this signals eternal life only for him. But because Jesus ascended into heaven, where he is even now seated at the right hand of God the Father, *he can bring us with him*. This is what the early church called the gospel.

The term "gospel" is used all the time, and there has even been a refreshing emphasis on "gospel-centrality" in many churches in the last few years. This is a good thing because the gospel is the centerpiece of the Christian faith. But sometimes when a term is frequently used, it becomes background noise. We find ourselves wondering, "what do we mean by that again?"

---

1   Peter Leithart, "Christian Novelty: What Homer Could Not See, & Jane Austen Could," in *Touchstone* (March 2005).

2   Quoted in Leithart.

3   Leithart.

4   This is central to the thesis of Ralph Wood, *The Comedy of Redemption: Christian Faith and Comic Vision in Four American Novelists* (South Bend, IN: Univ. of Notre Dame Press, 1991).

Christians borrowed the term "gospel" from broader culture. The word "gospel" (literally, "good news") was used technically to refer to news about Rome or the emperor. For example, when a new emperor ascended to power, a messenger would travel through the towns announcing the "good news" (gospel) of the ascension of this new ruler. We have to remember that when the writers of the New Testament and the early church were using the term gospel, they were talking about more than the forgiveness of sins. *They were talking about the coronation of a King!* Jesus has risen from the dead, but he also has ascended to the throne. He is the King![5]

Listen to the language Paul uses in Philippians: "Therefore God has highly exalted him and bestowed on him the name that is above every name, so that at the name of Jesus every knee should bow, in heaven and on earth and under the earth, and every tongue confess that Jesus Christ is Lord, to the glory of God the Father" (Philippians 2:9-11).

If what we confess in the Creed is true (that Jesus has been exalted over all things), then this gospel will make a real difference in this world. We should not be surprised that the ascension of Jesus leaves footprints in history; on the contrary, we should expect it. The Christian faith has changed literature, art, politics, and economics, and it will surely change your life, your direction, and your day. It is the reason why, in the aftermath of Hurricane Katrina, churches are virtually the only ones in New Orleans still building homes, while the media, Hollywood, and corporate America have long since gone home. Churches keep plugging along, and face all kinds of fears. We move toward the need because we know that our King rules. We can turn down the temptation to give in to materialism or lust, we can deny any darkness that has a pull on our heart, because we know that Christ is the one true King who rules all! His ascension makes a difference.

If you really believe that Jesus is exalted above all things, that he reigns as King, then it will change the trajectory of your life, the outcome of your story. Pastor Sandy Willson has said, "The greatest impediment to the mission of the church is not the evils outside of the church (in our culture and our city), but the cynicism and apathy inside the church."[6]

Jesus is alive, and he reigns as King. If you really believe this, your cynicism will start to melt away because you know he has the power and authority to make real change happen — in your city, and in the lives of the people around you. How pagan it is then when Christians cynically say of someone else, "they will never change. They are too far away from God to be helped." Jesus is alive! He ascended! He rules as King!

If you really believe this, your apathy will start to melt away. To know that Jesus is exalted, that he reigns, and that he will come again, gives us a hopeful

5 For an excellent treatment of this, see Brian Walsh and Sylvia Keesmaat, *Colossians Remixed: Subverting the Empire* (Downers Grove, IL: IVP, 2004).

6 Sandy Willson, in a sermon entitled "Jesus Christ, the Glory of the Church."

urgency to the cause of the gospel and the mission of the church. C.S. Lewis said, "There is a kind of happiness and wonder that makes you serious."[7] When you get a view of the glory of the resurrected and ascended Jesus, it makes you serious about his mission — because you want to serve the King.

But how can we say that this doctrine makes any difference in this world, when we confess that Jesus is departing for another? This is counterintuitive because the ascension of Jesus is the story of his *withdrawing* from our lives. Or is it? Luke would argue to the contrary. Because when we confess Jesus' ascension, we are confessing not only his exaltation, but — somewhat mysteriously — his presence with us.

THE PRESENCE OF JESUS

Notice what Jesus promises his disciples: "but you will receive power when the Holy Spirit has come upon you" (Acts 1:8). Earlier Jesus had told them, "These things I have spoken to you while I am still with you. But the Helper, the Holy Spirit, whom the Father will send in my name, he will teach you all things and bring to your remembrance all that I have said to you" (John 14:25-26).

The ascension of Jesus does *not* indicate the absence of God. Rather, God is *more* present to us now than he was to his disciples during Jesus' lifetime. We sometimes say, "I would believe, or I would obey God, if he was here the way he was in the Bible." But think about this: in the incarnation, Jesus merely stood *beside* his disciples. Now, by the power of the Holy Spirit, he dwells *within* them.

This is why the apostle Paul can say that Christians themselves are now the "temple of the living God" (II Corinthians 6:16), replacing the temple of Jerusalem, the holiest of places. When we confess that Jesus ascended into heaven, this comes with the promise of the Holy Spirit, who dwells in us (Romans 8:9-11). This means God is participating in our lives in a more intimate way than ever before.

Not long ago a Christian woman asked a pastor friend of mine (Ray) about angels. She said she believes God sends angels all around her at all times to minister to her. She asked if my pastor friend agreed. He answered by saying the Bible doesn't give us much information about how many angels there are, or how often they visit us. But he told her it doesn't really matter if we know the answer to this question, because we already have something even better. Not just angels, but God himself is present within all believers. The Holy Spirit dwells in Christians all the time.

God is present to us because, if you are a Christian, the "Spirit of God dwells in you" (Romans 8:9). But God is also present to us when we gather for worship. Jesus said to his disciples, "Where two or three are gathered in my name, there am I among them" (Matthew 18:20). When we gather together for worship there is a way in which we are actually participating in the ascension of Jesus.

---

7 C.S. Lewis, *The Last Battle* (New York, NY: HarperCollins, 1984), 212 .

A number of commentators point out that, in the Old Testament, ascension is a precondition for worship. Worship always takes place on the heights. For example:

- Abraham ascended Mount Moriah to offer his son on the altar
- Moses climbed Mount Sinai to meet God
- The sanctuaries of Israel were placed on the top of hills
- Every time worshippers went to the temple in Jerusalem, they were "going up" to God's house, ascending to worship

Jesus' ascent is a fulfillment of this pattern. The book of Hebrews tells us that he has ascended to the true sanctuary of heaven, towards which all earthly sanctuaries point. "For Christ has entered, not into holy places made with hands, which are copies of the true things, but into heaven itself, now to appear in the presence of God on our behalf" (Hebrews 9:24). And even more, in worship Jesus brings us with him. "But you have come to Mount Zion and to the city of the living God, the heavenly Jerusalem, and to innumerable angels in festal gathering" (Hebrews 12:22).

In some mysterious way our worship actually lifts us up to heaven! Jesus has ascended to the true sanctuary of heaven, and not only does he prepare a place for us there in the future, but even now we get to participate in that heavenly worship as we worship here on earth.

What difference does any of this make? For one thing, this makes Christianity different from any other religion or ideology. Other religions (or sociological movements) are based on the teachings of someone who is now dead (Buddha, Joseph Smith, Confucius). But not Christianity; Jesus is risen, reigning, and present in our lives.

Second, it gives Christians confidence when they pray. Why do you think God listens or cares when you pray? Pagan religions go through all kinds of elaborate gimmicks, formulas, and rituals in hopes that their prayers will be heard. This is why the ancient fertility religions had temple prostitution: to get the gods' attention. Maybe the attraction of live sex in the temple would cause the gods to take notice and listen to their prayers. But Hebrews 9 teaches that Christ has entered into heaven itself to appear in the presence of the Father on our behalf. Christ is in the presence of God — *for us*. He has been exalted so that those who trust in him and are united to him can have uninterrupted access to God the Father.

God did not leave us when Jesus ascended into heaven. God participates in our lives moment by moment in the person of the Holy Spirit. The early church boldly moved forward into mission because they were convinced of the presence of the Spirit in their lives, and that Jesus was interceding for them in heaven.

MISSION OF THE CHURCH

Notice the impact of the ascension on the disciples. They don't remain standing in the spot, slack-jawed, wondering at Christ being lifted up into heaven. The Book of Acts goes on to show us that the church immediately exploded into ministry. They plunged themselves into serving the world for which Christ died. They healed, they preached, they proclaimed the gospel of their ascended Lord in word and deed. The ascension did not reduce their commitment to this world; it greatly increased it. Why? Because of the last words they received from the Lord.

There are lots of famous last words.
- Julius Caesar: "*et tu Brute?*"
- Karl Marx: "Last words are for fools who haven't said enough."
- O. Henry: "Don't turn down the light. I am afraid to go home in the dark."
- Pablo Picasso: "Drink to me!"

But Jesus' last words surpass them all. His were the words, not of the dying, but of a risen King who was ascending to be at the Father's right hand, to rule the cosmos. In Acts 1:8 he gives them a charge, a set of instructions, blueprints for their life and mission. "You will be my witnesses in Jerusalem and in all Judea and Samaria, and to the ends of the earth." What does it mean to be a "witness"?

Witnesses Are Messengers

The apostles ask, "Lord, will you at this time restore the kingdom to Israel?" (Acts 1:6). It seems like an innocent enough question at first. But John Calvin comments, "There are as many errors in this question as words."[8]

Let's look at just a few problems. First, the verb, "restore." There is a good and biblical way to use the terms restore and restoration. We know that when Jesus comes again, he will restore the world; Revelation 21:5 says that he will make "all things new." But what the disciples have in mind is something different. They are thinking of the earthly fortunes of Israel. They may be thinking of the "good old days" a few centuries prior when Judas Maccabeus led the Israelite nation in revolt against the Greeks. They were hoping that Jesus would lead the same kind of revolt against the Romans. The apostles are thinking, "We are finally going to get revenge for all the injustice that has been done to us."

But Jesus says, "You are going to be my witnesses." Not my revolutionaries, not my politicians, not my soldiers. The kingdom is going to expand, but not through violence and coercion. Instead, it's going to come through proclamation and demonstration.

A second error in the disciples' question in verse 6 is in the noun, "Israel." Again, they are thinking of God building an earthly kingdom, a powerful nation that would stand for God. But Jesus tells them that they will be his witnesses in

---

8 John Calvin, *The Acts of the Apostles, Vol.1* (Grand Rapids, MI: Wm. B. Eerdmans, 1995), 29.

Jerusalem, Judea, Samaria (Israel's neighbors who were culturally and racially different), and even to the ends of the earth. The Kingdom of God is cross-cultural, multi-national, and multi-ethnic. We see this story playing out in the book of Acts, as the church is scattered through persecution and Christian communities began to pop up all over the Mediterranean world. And the church is not content to remain Hebrew, but quickly begins to take the message to the Gentiles around them.

A third error in the disciples' question is in the adverbial phrase "at this time." "Jesus, are you going to do this *at this time?*" What does Jesus say in response? "It is not for you to know times or seasons that the Father has fixed by his own authority."

While in graduate school I (Josh) was a teaching assistant for an undergraduate class called "Apocalyptic Literature." Though it was long before we got to know one another, my wife was a student in the class; she still hasn't forgiven me for the B+ she received.[9]

One of the texts for the class was a book by Paul Boyer called *When Time Shall Be No More.* Boyer read hundreds of apocalyptic novels written by evangelicals in the 20th century, and found that they all had one thing in common: every one of them was wrong about the end of the world. "It is not for you to know times or seasons," Jesus says; those apocalyptic writers would have been wise to listen to him.

We are *not* to equate the Kingdom with our nation. We are *not* to try to usher the kingdom in with force. And we are *not* to speculate about the end of the world. But we *are* called to be witnesses — messengers of the kingdom, declaring and demonstrating the gospel to our neighbors, our friends, our city.

Witnesses are Martyrs

The Greek word for witness is the same word that is used for "martyr." A martyr is someone who suffers for their cause. Don't miss the force of this. The disciples would not be generals in a conquering kingdom. They would be martyrs! They would suffer and sacrifice for the cause of their King.

Colossians 1:24 gives us some perspective on this. Paul writes, "Now I rejoice in my sufferings for your sake, and in my flesh I am filling up what is lacking in Christ's afflictions for the sake of his body, that is, the church." What could Paul mean when he says he is filling up what is lacking in Christ's afflictions? He does not mean that somehow Christ's suffering is deficient in its worth or value. The Bible says time and again that Christ's suffering is the perfect once and for all sacrifice for sins. So what could Paul have in mind?

---

9 She maintains she deserved at least an A-. That is easily the most costly B+ I ever gave out.

What he means is that there's nothing lacking in Christ's sufferings, except the presentation of his sufferings to a watching world. John Piper explains it this way:

> God intends for the afflictions of Christ to be presented to the world through the afflictions of his people. God really means for the body of Christ, the church, to experience some of the suffering he experienced so that when we proclaim the cross as the way to life, people will see the marks of the cross in us and feel the love of the cross from us. Our calling is to make Christ real for people by the afflictions we experience in bringing them the message of salvation.[10]

The gospel isn't going to be brought to the world through a kind of triumphalism. It will go out as Christians are willing to suffer, to lay down their lives in bringing the good news to their neighbors, to their friends, and to the nations.

J. Oswald Sanders tells the story of an indigenous Indian missionary who walked barefoot from village to village preaching the gospel. After a long day and many miles and much discouragement, he tried to speak up for the gospel in one particular village. They shouted him down and ran him out. Dejected and exhausted, he slouched down under a tree and fell asleep.

> When he awoke the whole town was gathered to hear him. The head man of the village explained that they came to look him over while he was sleeping. When they saw his blistered feet they concluded he must be a holy man, and that they had been evil to reject him. And according to Sanders, the whole village believed.[11]

That is a dramatic example, but the principle is true in your life as well — God's work happens through sacrifice. The Kingdom expands when you lay down your life, when you sacrifice your desires and your comfort for the good of others. Practically, this means investing time and effort in building relationships with people. For some of you (introverts especially) this is risky and uncomfortable. But this is Kingdom work. It means dealing with difficult people, and bearing their burdens as you seek to comfort and help and encourage. It means sacrificing time and emotional energy to regularly be on your knees in prayer for the people that God has brought across your path.

Do you see yourself as a witness, as a messenger, as a martyr? If you are connected to Jesus by faith, then this is what you are called to be. And even more, it is part of your identity whether you know it or not. When you are united to Christ, witness is not just something you do; it is who you are.

When you experience the forgiveness of Jesus Christ, you become a person who forgives and you give people a glimpse of a future where things are made right. When you believe in the ascension of Jesus Christ and honor him with your time, talents, and money, you witness to his Kingship. You declare that you

---

10 John Piper, *Desiring God* (Sisters, OR: Multnomah, 1986), 225.

11 We first heard this in Piper's address called "Doing Missions When Dying Is Gain." It also is in his book *Let the Nations be Glad* (Grand Rapids, MI: Baker Academic, 2003), 94-95.

are not King, and that he is the real Lord and King over your life. When you trust in his sacrifice for you, you become the type of person who considers nothing your own, but are willing to give everything away. When you believe that he is the risen King, you know you can face any fear you might have in your mission (the crime, the secularism, the fear of not being received warmly) for nothing is bigger than his kingship.

Back to our opening image. Your life doesn't have to be a tragedy. It can be a comedy. You can laugh when the curtain falls. You can make footprints in history. This happens when you truly believe and live in the light of the Kingship of Jesus Christ.

STUDY QUESTIONS:

- Does your church and family celebrate Ascension Sunday (40 days after Easter)? How can remembering the Christian calendar give meaning and a holy rhythm to our days?

- Do you see life as more tragic or comic? How does the ascension enable us to laugh in the face of challenges and opposition?

- What does the term "gospel" mean to you? Is the good news only about Jesus' atonement, or does it also involve his ascending to heaven to rule as King?

- Do you find yourself hampered in your mission by cynicism or apathy? Do the Creed and Acts 1 provide a remedy?

- Do you agree that the ascension is not about Jesus withdrawing, but about him drawing even closer to his children? Why?

- If worship lifts us up to heaven and ushers us into God's presence, what does that say about its place in our week and in our lives?

- Do you find yourself bored in your prayer life? Shy? Neglectful? If Christ is now in the presence of the Father for believers, interceding on our behalf, what does this mean for your prayer life?

- Even after the resurrection, the apostles themselves show they don't yet fully understand Jesus' role. Clearly, they were still expecting him to restore self-rule and theocracy for the nation of Israel. Instead, God was calling them beyond narrow national interests to serving their neighbors (both Jew and Greek) and going out to the ends of the earth in mission. Do you see any connections here with those who sometimes seemed more concerned with restoring political authority to Christians than with serving their neighbors missionally?

- If witnesses (martyrs) are to present Christ's sufferings to the world to serve their neighbors, how do you see that happening in your life? What does that mean for you specifically, regarding word and deed? How do you present Christ's sufferings to your kids as you shepherd them? Or your parents? To difficult people at work? How is it reflected in your lifestyle choices: the kind of neighborhood you choose to live in, your distance from and interaction with the poor, your chastity, your career choices?

- What do you fear? Can embracing Jesus' ascension and kingship empower you to face your fears with boldness? Do you need others in the body to lock arms with you now and help you, by directing your gaze back to King Jesus in your fears? Are there others in the church that you can encourage today to face their fears by reminding them that Christ is King? Who?

He Will Come to Judge

CHAPTER 8

¹O sing to the LORD a new
song, for he has done
marvelous things!
His right hand and his holy arm
have worked salvation for him.
²The LORD has made
known his salvation; he has
revealed his righteousness in the sight of the nations.
³He has remembered his steadfast love and faithfulness
to the house of Israel.
All the ends of the earth have seen the salvation of our God.
⁴Make a joyful noise to the LORD, all the earth; break
forth into joyous song and sing praises!
⁵Sing praises to the LORD with the lyre, with the lyre and the sound of melody!
⁶With trumpets and the sound of the horn make a
joyful noise before the King, the LORD!
⁷Let the sea roar, and all that fills it; the world and those who dwell in it!
⁸Let the rivers clap their hands; let the hills sing for joy together
⁹before the LORD, for he comes to judge the earth.
He will judge the world with righteousness, and the peoples with equity.
Psalm 98

Psalm 98 is a praise song, and one with which you are probably at least a little familiar. This is the text on which the Christmas carol "Joy to the World" is based. One way to view the structure of the psalm is as ever-expanding worship of God. In verses 1-3, it's *the people of God (Israel)* who are invited to worship. In verses 4-6, it gets bigger — *people from all over the earth* are invited to worship God. By the time we get to verse 7, it's not just people, but *all of creation* is worshipping God. "Let the sea roar...let the rivers clap."

We might also look at this psalm as giving us reasons why we should come to worship God. Verses 1-3 tell us to worship God *because he is the Savior*: "His right hand and his holy arm have worked salvation for him." Verses 4-6 invite us to worship God *because he is the King*: "Make a joyful noise before the King." Verses 7-9 tell us to worship God because *he is the Judge*: "He will judge the world with righteousness / and the peoples with equity."

It is easy to see how you can sing praises about God the Savior, or about God the King. But what does it mean to worship Jesus as the one "who will come again to judge the living and the dead"? Or, to put it another way, is the idea of God's judgment of the world really good news?

AN UNCOMFORTABLE CONCEPT

Leaving aside apocalyptic movies and the taunts of professional wrestlers, the notion of Judgment Day is not all that popular. And yet, it appears all over the Bible. We might immediately think of the Old Testament, which regularly speaks about "the Day of the Lord." There are some who will object, rejecting what they see as the primitive teachings of the Old Testament in favor of the "gentler" teaching of the New Testament. But think about these New Testament texts:

- John 9:39: "For judgment I [Jesus] came into this world..."
- II Corinthians 5:10: "For we must all appear before the judgment seat of Christ, so that each one may receive what is due for what he has done in the body, whether good or evil."
- Revelation 19:11,15-16: "Then I saw heaven opened, and behold, a white horse! The one sitting on it is called Faithful and True, and in righteousness he judges and makes war... He will tread the winepress of the fury of the wrath of God the Almighty. On his robe and on his thigh he has a name written, King of kings and Lord of lords."[1]

There are several reasons we shy away from the New Testament's teachings on judgment. To begin with, we're uncomfortable with the idea of God as a judge. The language of judgment makes modern people wince. Dennis Prager, a Jewish thinker, notes that in our culture, "*judging* evil is widely considered worse than *doing* evil."[2]

Of course, this aversion to the language of judgment is not altogether surprising. After all, many of us have been the victims of unfair judgment. People who don't care about us, or don't know us or our circumstances, pronounce verdicts on our lives. These people seem to only care about rules, rules that they usually make up themselves. The rules often become more important than the people themselves. Sadly, this happens in a lot of churches. And these abusive attitudes and behaviors make us jumpy when we hear anything that even hints at judgment.

The irony, of course, is that hating all forms of judgment ends up being itself a new form of judgmentalism. Those who make any judgments on any issue are judged by the people who don't believe in judgment! We judge people for judging people, without seeing that we're doing the same thing.

---

1   The great Johnny Cash has a couple of songs based on these verses.
2   Dennis Prager, "The Sin of Forgiveness," *The Wall Street Journal* (December 15, 1997).

So we are intolerant of a God who judges. But we are even more uncomfortable with a God who might judge us. It is offensive to think about God judging anyone, but it's downright unbearable to think about God judging *us*.

Several years ago *The Atlantic Monthly* cited a study from the Barna Research Group showing that while 71% of Americans believe people will go to hell, just .005% (5 one-thousandths of a percent) think they themselves are in real danger of going there.[3] There are 85,000 people that live within a three-mile radius of my (Josh's) neighborhood in Cincinnati. Using these figures, this means just four people think they are going to hell. If what the Bible says about judgment is true, that figure might be a bit low. What does Jesus say? "The gate is wide and the way is easy that leads to destruction, and those who enter by it are many" (Matthew 7:13). But if we are intolerant of the idea of a judging God, this becomes extremely difficult to believe.

But the Bible teaches this is not a truth to minimize or apologize for. Rather, it is actually somehow good news. The Psalmist sings with joy ("make a joyful noise") that God is Judge. God's coming again to judge the living and the dead is somehow good news! Psalm 98 is upbeat about it. How is that in any way possible?

GOOD NEWS FOR THOSE SINNED AGAINST

The oppressed, those who have been hurt, need a judging God if they are to have any hope and joy. We need and want a God who will make things right; judgment is bound up in the process of justice.

In the novel *Original Sin* by P.D. James, Kate (one of the main characters), says to her Jewish colleague:

> There were a dozen different religions among the children at [my school]. We seemed always to be celebrating some kind of feast or ceremony. Usually it required making a noise and dressing up. The official line was that all religions were equally important. I must say that the result was to leave me with the conviction that they were equally unimportant. I suppose if you don't teach religion with conviction it becomes just one more boring subject. Perhaps I'm a natural pagan. I don't go in for all this emphasis on sin, suffering and judgment. If I had a God I'd like Him to be intelligent, cheerful and amusing.
>
> Her colleague replied:
>
> I doubt whether you'd find [such a god] much of a comfort when they herded you into the gas chambers. You might prefer a god of vengeance.[4]

Don't dismiss the Christian faith because it contains teachings about judgment; to do so would be to abandon real hope in life. There is a desire for justice

---

3 "Hell is for Other People," *The Atlantic Monthly* (http://www.theatlantic.com/past/docs/ issues/2004/01/primarysources.htm).

4 P.D. James, *Original Sin* (New York, NY: Warner, 1994), 232.

and equity deep within you. This is why we cheer in movies when the bad guy gets what he deserves, or when we hear that an arrest has been made for the murder that happened last week in your city. It is the reason we rage against the system when we feel we've been taken advantage of. It is the reason that the language of individual and human rights is so prominent in our political discourse.

A just God is the only hope millions of people have. There are people who suffer severe injustices today. Just one example: the commercial sex trade is a $32 billion per year industry. Each year, nearly two million children are exploited and trafficked in the commercial sex trade. Twenty-seven million men, women and children are held as slaves.[5]

All of us have experienced persecution or injustice to one degree or another. All of us have been sinned against. The doctrine of God's judgment is the only reason for hope that one day things will be made right. Without a final judgment, the books will never be balanced.

But there is far more to think about here. God's judgment is not just good news for those who have been sinned against. It also can bring joy to sinners.

GOOD NEWS FOR SINNERS

The whole tenor of Psalm 98 is joy. "O sing to the Lord a new song!... Make a joyful noise to the Lord... let the hills sing for joy for he comes to judge." Why should we who are being judged rejoice?

We Rejoice Because God Judges in Love

"He has remembered his steadfast love and faithfulness to the house of Israel" (Psalm 98:3). God's love is never set against his judgment. Both work together. God is not fickle; he does not have "good" or "bad" days, nor do his love and justice depend on his mood. God is completely consistent in his character. His love and justice work together.

This makes all the difference in the world when we think about God's judgment. "His right hand and his holy arm have worked salvation..." (Psalm 98:2). Isaiah 40 uses the same imagery for the way God works. "Behold, the Lord comes with might, and *his arm rules for him*" (Isaiah 40:10). "He will tend his flock like a shepherd; *he will gather the lambs in his arms*" (Isaiah 40:11). The same Hebrew word for "arm" is used in both verses 10 and 11. The arm that rules and judges (Isaiah 40:10) is the arm that gathers the lambs (Isaiah 40:11). The arm of God that rules with justice is the arm that has scooped us up in his love and faithfulness.

The first sign that parents don't love their kids enough is when they let them get away with anything, when they refuse to discipline and want to only to be their pals. God refuses to do this because he loves his children. He judges his people in loving discipline. That is good news. But there's more.

---

5   The source for these statistics is the website of the International Justice Mission (http://www.ijm.org/ourwork/injusticetoday).

We Rejoice Because God Judges With Perfect Righteousness

"He will judge the earth with righteousness, and the peoples with equity" (Psalm 98:9). What does this mean? For one thing, it means that when God judges, he knows all the extenuating circumstances in our lives.

Alister McGrath tells a story about shepherds in East Anglia, the center of England's wool trade in the Middle Ages.

> When a shepherd died, he would be buried in a coffin packed full of wool. The idea was that when the Day of Judgment came, Jesus would see the wool and realize that this man had been a shepherd. As he himself had once been a shepherd, he would know the pressures the man had faced — the amount of time needed to look after wayward sheep and so on — and would understand why he hadn't been to church much![6]

So much of our skittishness about God's judgment is because we have seen the imperfections of human judgment. We are all too familiar with wrong verdicts based on imperfect knowledge. Even the best people and best governments don't know everything, and can wrongfully accuse, try, and sentence innocent people. And sometimes, even if a person is truly guilty, their punishment does not fit their crime.

This is never the case with God. We can rejoice in him as Judge, because he judges with perfect righteousness and equity. There is no unfairness in God! Nothing is hidden from his eyes. He knows all the extenuating circumstances in your life. He knows your family background and how that affects you. He knows about abuse that's affected the way you relate to people. He knows when you've felt cornered and out of options. Rejoice, therefore, because he judges justly and equitably, and with everything in view!

However, this also poses a problem. We can convince ourselves that all our problems are the result of things that happen to us, or are caused by other people's mistakes and sins. We might be able to convince other people of that as well, and perhaps we can convince ourselves of our innocence for a time. But God, the all-knowing, perfectly righteous Judge, knows all sides of the story. He knows the bad things that have been done to us, but he also knows all the bad things we have eagerly chosen. He knows all our evil, in our actions, thoughts, and attitudes. He sees it all. There is no escaping the Righteous Judge and his knowledge of us. The Psalmist prays, "O Lord, you have searched me and known me! You know when I sit down and when I rise up; you discern my thoughts from afar... Where shall I go from your Spirit? Or where shall I flee from your presence?" (Psalm 139:1, 7).

If this isn't disconcerting, then you probably aren't quite getting it. If you have been in a truly intimate relationship, you know that the better people know you, the riskier the relationship becomes. It is for this reason that a lot of people avoid intimacy and move from one relationship to another. You may not be

6 McGrath, *I Believe*, 77-78.

able to handle being known because it's too threatening. This is why some folks bounce from church to church as well. We don't want to be found out.

If human relationships are threatening, how much more fearful is a relationship with an all-righteous divine Judge who knows everything about you? It ought to make you tremble and cry out for mercy. But that leads us to the best part of Psalm 98: judgment and salvation go hand in hand.

We Rejoice Because God's Judgment Saves

"[F]or he comes to judge the earth. He will judge the world in righteousness" (Psalm 98:9). The psalm ends on a note of judgment, but look where it begins: "[H]e has done marvelous things! His right hand and his holy arm have worked salvation for him. The Lord has made known his salvation..." (Psalm 98:1).

The psalmist begins by describing God as the Divine Warrior who has battled to bring salvation to his people. In doing so, he also brings judgment. This is often the case in the Biblical narrative. To save Israel from slavery in the exodus, he judges Egypt. To save his people from captivity, he judges the nations. *Salvation for some means judgment for others.*

The psalmist cheers because salvation is not just something in the past, but something that can be hoped for in the future. But the surprise ending is how God will bring this about. Who will be judged so that the people are set free?

John 19 describes the arrest and trial of Jesus. "[Pilate] brought Jesus out and sat down on the judgment seat...[and] delivered [Jesus] over to be crucified" (John 19:13). Jesus, the perfectly sinless Son of God, is judged and handed over. As Karl Barth famously noted, Jesus is "the Judge who was judged for us."[7]

This might cause us to be more startled than comforted. To that end, the *Heidelberg Catechism* asks, "What comfort is there that Christ shall come to judge?" Answer: "That the one who comes to judge is the very same person who previously came to be judged for my sake and has removed all curse from me."[8]

It is because God has judged Jesus that you can be saved. The good news that we sing about in our hymns, read about in the Bible, and confess in the Creed is that the very one who will one day come to *bring* judgment is the one who came to *bear* judgment. This is why John can say, "If we confess our sins, he is faithful and just to forgive us our sins and to cleanse us from all unrighteousness" (I John 1:9). It is because God has judged Jesus that you can be saved.

What is the upshot of all this? If you really believe that Jesus will come again to judge, how does it change your life?

First, you will make sure you are right with God. In the immortal words of Officer Tia from *Police Women of Cincinnati*: "if you're always ready, you don't need to get ready."[9]

---

7 Karl Barth, *Church Dogmatics* IV/1, tr. Geoffrey W. Bromiley, (Edinburgh: Clark, 1956), 211.
8 Our paraphrase of Q 52.
9 *Police Women of Cincinnati* was a short-lived and much-maligned reality TV show. It was popular for the younger members of New City Presbyterian Church in Cincinnati, mostly

Are you ready to meet Jesus? If you're not a follower of Christ, then this is the most important thing for you as you read this chapter. The Creed and the Scriptures teach that he will come again to judge the living and the dead. Your greatest need is to get ready to meet him.

He will judge with righteousness and equity, but every one of us will be found rightly guilty of rebellion against God (Romans 3:23). The only way to stand up under this judgment is to be united to Jesus by faith (Ephesians 2:8-9). Romans 6:23 tells us that the wages of sin is death; either you will pay for your own sin, or Jesus will. "Whoever hears my word and believes him who sent me has eternal life. He does not come into *judgment*, but has passed from death to life" (John 5:24).

Second, if you really believe in the judgment of God, then you won't feel the need to make yourself the judge. This is a tremendously liberating idea. If God is the Judge, then you don't need to be.

Some of us believe, at least at the practical level, that we need to discover everyone else's wrongs and pronounce judgment on them. We think that if we don't do it, no one will. And so we scrutinize and fixate on anything we find wrong in our friends, family, coworkers, and neighbors, and we tell others about the flaws we've found.[10]

It is true that we are called to contend for the truth and invite people to repent of sin, but some of us are obsessed in looking for wrongs in others. This produces a lack of charity and humility, and doesn't do any good at actually leading people to repentance. This obsession stems from the delusion that we must be the judge. It is evidence of a lack of faith that God will actually do his job and judge the world.

Even more personally, believing that God is Judge frees you up to give over your anger, to surrender your desire for revenge. If you don't believe in a God of judgment who metes out justice and one day will make all wrongs right, then you are always going to look for revenge. You will feel it is incumbent upon you to settle the score. But belief in the righteous, perfect judgment of God can enable you to lay down your anger and break the cycle of violence and retaliation.

Miroslav Volf, the Croatian philosopher and Yale professor, explains it this way:

> The practice of non-violence requires a belief in divine vengeance... My thesis will be unpopular with many in the West... But imagine speaking to people (as I have) whose cities and villages have been first plundered, then burned, and leveled to the ground, whose daughters and sisters have been raped, whose fathers and brothers have had their throats slit... Your point to them — we should not retaliate? Why not? I say

---

as an object of ridicule.

10 This is the subject of so many blogs — fault-finding in others. Some Christians seem especially adept at vitriolic rants against the perceived errors found in other Christians and churches.

— the only means of prohibiting violence by us is to insist that violence is only legitimate when it comes from God... Violence thrives today, secretly nourished by the belief that God refuses to take the sword... It takes the quiet of a suburb for the birth of the thesis that human non-violence is a result of a God who refuses to judge. In a scorched land — soaked in the blood of the innocent, the idea will invariably die, like other pleasant captivities of the liberal mind... if God were NOT angry at injustice and deception and did NOT make a final end of violence, that God would not be worthy of our worship.[11]

You can give your anger to God, because you can trust him as the perfect and righteous Judge, one who will bring justice and make all wrongs right.

Last, if you really believe Psalm 98, you will sing joyfully and loudly to the Lord. Both of us are pastors of Presbyterian churches. While Presbyterians tend to be active thinkers, we are not always joyful worshippers. This is a tragedy, because good theology should lead to great doxology.

Psalm 98 helps us here. The psalmist gives us lots of content and information about God: he is the Savior, the King, and the righteous Judge. But the psalmist won't stop there. It's not enough to think rightly. This must lead to worship! And we must do so loudly and joyfully! Good theology should always translate into great doxology. Right thoughts about God ought to always turn into joyful worship of God.

"*Make a joyful noise to the LORD, all the earth; break forth into joyous song and sing praises! Sing praises to the LORD with the lyre, with the lyre and the sound of melody! With trumpets and the sound of the horn make a joyful noise before the King, the LORD!*" (Psalm 98:4-6).

This psalm was first sung as a part of Old Testament worship in the temple. One scholar says, "The noise of temple worship was legendary."[12] Ezra 3 says that at times the joyful shouting in worship was so loud it could be heard far away.

When you go to church this Sunday, apply the counsel of Methodist pastor John Wesley.

Sing lustily, and with good courage. Beware of singing as if you were half dead or asleep; but lift up your voice with strength. Be no more afraid of your voice now, no more ashamed of its being heard, then when you sang [bar songs].[13]

Think of the way you sing karaoke in the bar, or the way you sing along at a rock concert. You ought to sing *at least* that loud, and with as much joy, this Sunday in church. As the psalmist says, "Make a joyful noise to the Lord!"

---

11 Miroslav Volf, *Exclusion and Embrace* (Nashville, TN: Abingdon, 1996), 303.

12 Marvin E. Tate, quoted in James Montgomery Boice, *Psalms, Vol. 2* (Grand Rapids, MI: Baker Books, 1996), 800.

13 Wesley, quoted in Boice, 800.

STUDY QUESTIONS:

- How can the thought of God's perfect judgment be a comfort in times when you are oppressed?

- Do you think you can hide things from God?

- In what ways is God's ultimate, perfect judgment good news?

- How can a firm confidence in God's judgment help overcome temptations to judge others?

- What do you think of Dr. Volf's quote? Do you think there are differences on this issue between the ethics of the state and those of individuals?

- What are the differences between making judgments and being judgmental?

- Are there ways that you need to repent of standing in judgment of certain people or groups?

- How can your church be a place that displays this biblical view of judgment?

The Holy Spirit

CHAPTER 9

[5]"If you love me, you will keep my commandments. [16]And I will ask the Father, and he will give you another Helper, to be with you forever, [17]even the Spirit of truth, whom the world cannot receive, because it neither sees him nor knows him. You know him, for he dwells with you and will be in you.

[18]"I will not leave you as orphans; I will come to you. [19]Yet a little while and the world will see me no more, but you will see me. Because I live, you also will live. [20]In that day you will know that I am in my Father, and you in me, and I in you. [21]Whoever has my commandments and keeps them, he it is who loves me. And he who loves me will be loved by my Father, and I will love him and manifest myself to him." [22]Judas (not Iscariot) said to him, "Lord, how is it that you will manifest yourself to us, and not to the world?" [23]Jesus answered him, "if anyone loves me, he will keep my word, and my Father will love him, and we will come to him and make our home with him. [24]Whoever does not love me does not keep my words. And the word that you hear is not mine but the Father's who sent me.

[25]"These things I have spoken to you while I am still with you. [26]But the Helper, the Holy Spirit, whom the Father will send in my name, he will teach you all things and bring to your remembrance all that I have said to you.

John 14:15-26

The Apostles' Creed is broken into three sections: I believe in God the Father; I believe in Jesus Christ, his Son; and lastly, I believe in the Holy Spirit. Christians believe that God is Trinitarian in his very nature.[1] He exists in three Persons. This can be a very difficult concept to understand because the Bible does not teach that there are three gods. "Hear, O Israel: the Lord our God, the Lord is one" (Deuteronomy 6:4). But it does speak of three Persons within the godhead: God the Father is clearly God;[2] Jesus, the Son, is God;[3] and the Holy Spirit is God.[4]

---

1 For a fuller description of the Trinity, see chapter 3.
2 John 6:27, I Corinthians 8:6, Ephesians 5:20, James 1:27, I Peter 1:2, II Peter 1:17,
3 Isaiah 9:6, John 1:1-4, Romans 9:5, Colossians 2:9, Titus 2:13, II Peter 1:1.
4 Psalm 139:7-8, Matthew 28:19, Acts 5:3-4, I Corinthians 2:10-11, 3:16.

We come now to this third part of the Apostles' Creed. What does it mean to confess, "I believe in the Holy Spirit"? There are myriad ways in which people understand the Holy Spirit and his work in our lives. There are some people (and some churches) who appear to talk only about the Holy Spirit and nothing else. They claim that God speaks regularly and specifically, even down to the smallest details, like which socks they should wear. I (Josh) had a friend in seminary who regularly said, "the Holy Spirit told me to go to this coffee shop, or take a left on this street, or ask out this girl."

There is a danger in this kind of thinking. For one thing, when you over-spiritualize, you begin to equate God's voice with your feelings. That's not a good place to be. Our feelings ebb and flow and are at times contradictory, but God is not a God of confusion (I Corinthians 14:33). He is consistent in what he tells us.

Claiming a specific "word from the Spirit" can also be manipulative. When I tell you that God has spoken to me directly about your life and you disagree with me, I put you in the unenviable position of disagreeing not only with me, but with God himself.

But there are dangers on the other side, too. Many Christians (and churches) rarely mention the Holy Spirit. There's an old joke about the Trinity deciding on vacation plans for Spring Break. The Father decides he'd like to go to the mountains, since they reflect his majesty and power. The Son desires to go back to his old stomping grounds in Palestine. The Spirit decides to go to a Presbyterian church, because he wanted to go someplace he'd never been before. We tease (as Presbyterian pastors ourselves), but the point is, there are Christians of all denominations who simply don't know what to do with the doctrine of the Holy Spirit. We know he is in the Bible, and we say we believe in him, but we have no real framework for how he works in our life. And so our *functional trinity* — the trinity in which we actually believe — is the Father, Son, and the Holy Bible.

But the Apostles' Creed is a check against this tendency, reminding us of the importance of the work of the Spirit. John 14 teaches us about the crucial role of the Spirit in the life of the church, and every individual believer.

I (Ray) remember when my daughter was learning to ride her bike. Her first bike had training wheels and she was extremely wary as she learned to ride. She wanted to know that her mom or dad was there for her, next to her, able to catch her if she fell. But soon she got the hang of it and would zip around Audubon Park fearlessly. She expertly weaved in between strangers and whipped around unsuspecting people who were just trying to have a nice stroll. She became fearless on her bike once she got the hang of it.

When she was six years old we removed her training wheels, and suddenly everything was different. The idea of riding her bike suddenly brought dread. She was unsure of herself and very unstable again. Anyone who has ever met Rachel will tell you that she hates to be out of control. She soon got the hang of it again, but for a while when we'd go to the same park to ride, she wanted to know that my wife or I were right there next to her in case she wiped out.

New Orleans, where I minister, is a city like that. The ups and downs of our great city are such that we get good news and bad news almost every day, often at the same time. Like my daughter on her bike, we feel like our city and our culture could tip over and wipe out any minute. Is there anyone there to steady our ride? The disciples in John 14 are in a very similar situation. At first they were a little uncertain of Jesus. Why is he hanging out with drunks and degenerates all the time, and blowing off all the religious leaders and important people? They wondered why Jesus had a different view of the rules than the priests and the theologians of the day. But soon they began to understand. They started to get what he was doing. They traveled all over Israel with him, watching him do amazing feats, and they eventually became comfortable with Jesus as their leader and with their roles as his followers.

But just when they were feeling like they were in a good groove, Jesus dropped a bombshell on them. He announced that he would be going away. He was leaving them. Can you imagine what they must have been feeling? They had given up everything to follow him: jobs, homes, security, comfort. And now Jesus is saying that he will be leaving, and they're terrified all over again. The training wheels are off.

This is the context for Jesus' teaching about the Holy Spirit in John 14. He offers them comfort, but he doesn't do it by saying, "Don't worry. You're going to do fine without me." He doesn't tell them that their training will serve them well, or that he has nothing left to teach them because they are as prepared as they ever will be. No, instead Jesus says, "Don't worry. I'm sending you the Holy Spirit, who will be with you, and live in you." We learn five very important things about the Holy Spirit from this text, which inform what we mean when we confess with the Creed, "I believe in the Holy Spirit."

THE SPIRIT IS A HE, NOT AN IT

The Holy Spirit is a Person, not an entity or an impersonal force. "[H]e will give you another Helper, to be with you forever, even the Spirit of truth, *whom* the world cannot receive, because it neither sees *him* nor knows *him*" (John 14:16-17). Note the personal pronouns used to describe the Spirit.

The Bible repeatedly testifies to the personal nature of the Holy Spirit. Ephesians 4:30 tells us the Spirit can be grieved. He can be outraged, according to Hebrews 10:29. Romans 15:30 says that the Spirit loves. These are the characteristics of a personal being, so when you think of the Holy Spirit, you need to understand you are interacting with a person.

How you understand the Spirit's nature will affect the way you relate to him. The Bible commands us to walk by the Spirit and be filled with the Spirit. How are we to do that? If you have an impersonal understanding of the Spirit, if you believe he is merely a force in the universe, then you're going to relate to the Spirit in a mechanical way — perhaps like the Jedi in *Star Wars*. If you tap into "the force" in the right way, you can bend its power to your will. Eastern thought says that if you can posture yourself correctly through a spiritual regimen, formula, or meditation, then you can get the power of the forces of the universe to work through you.

But this is not the Christian understanding of the Holy Spirit. Because the Spirit is a Person, our interaction with him is not about pushing the right buttons or changing the environmental conditions. Belief in the Holy Spirit means growing a relationship with a person. It is about getting to know someone, so that over time you begin to think like he thinks, feel like he feels, and act like he acts.

Are you trying to get to know the Spirit? Are you communing with him through prayer? Do you enter into his presence in worship and Bible reading? Are you asking him to work in your life and the life of your friends and your church?

The Holy Spirit is a person — a "he," not an "it." And that person is fully God.

THE SPIRIT IS DIVINE

This is another way of declaring that the Spirit is God himself, and it is the only way that Jesus' words could be of any comfort to the disciples. Jesus tells them he is going away, but he wants to assure them that they are not losing God's presence in their lives. Don't worry, because the Spirit is coming to you.

"I will ask the Father and he will give you another Helper" (John 14:16). Take note of the word "another." There are two different words used in the New Testament that are often translated "another." The first is the word *hetero*, which means "opposed, or different," as in the word "heterosexual." But the second word translated as "another" is the Greek word used here. It is the word *allos*, which means "just like the former."

Jesus can tell the disciples not to worry because another Helper "just like him" is coming. Someone with the same essence, the same nature, the same mission would be with them. The coming Holy Spirit would be of the exact same divine essence as Jesus Christ.

That is why this is good news for the disciples. Jesus was leaving, but it didn't mean that the presence of God would be gone from them forever. In fact, Jesus was saying that God would be even more intimately present to them. When Jesus walked the earth, he merely *stood by* his disciples. But now in the Spirit, God will *live in* his disciples.

THE SPIRIT LIVES IN HIS PEOPLE

In verse 23, Jesus talks about the presence of God in the life of a believer. He says that he and the Father (by the Spirit) "will love him and come to him and make our home with him" (John 14:23). The apostle Paul makes it even more clear in II

Corinthians 3:16: "Do you not know that you are God's temple and that God's Spirit dwells in you?" God's people, the church, is the new temple of God. He has come to dwell in his people.

This has tremendous implications for how you understand and live your life. Think about what happens when you have a visitor to your home. You immediately clean the place up — everyone's house looks its best when company is coming over. For once, you actually want to clean, because you care about this person. You want to give them the red carpet treatment.

When you have important company over, the changes are more pervasive than the relative cleanliness of your house. You actually begin to think and act differently while they are staying with you. You are less concerned about yourself and more interested in the welfare of your honored guest.

There is also joy in their presence. The house is a little brighter, the meals are more cheerful. There is more laughter and more stories. Little things don't matter as much. To sum up, your life is transformed by their coming in.

This is how it is with the Holy Spirit. If you are aware of the Spirit's presence in your life, it changes everything. It transforms how you act, what you say, how you spend your time. If you really believe he has come in and, as Jesus says, made his home with you, it changes your life.

Tim Keller tells the story of a man he counseled who had an affair.[5] He had a mistress for a number of years, and eventually it all came to light. It wrecked his life and his marriage. While the affair was going on, his wife would sometimes travel for work. And he would have his mistress come to the house. But when he did, he had to go through the house before she got there and turn over all the pictures of his wife. The very presence of her picture affected what he could and couldn't do. It affected his behavior.

If you are a Christian, do you know that God is living in your life? The Holy Spirit has made his home in you. There are probably things that you are doing right now that you wouldn't be doing if you really believed that. When no one else is looking, the Holy Spirit is right there with you. When you balance your checkbook, when you watch TV, when you surf the internet, when you go on dates, the Holy Spirit is there. He lives inside you. We don't mean to scare you — this is actually good news. But it ought to be a little sobering as well.

This is especially the case because the person of the Holy Spirit who dwells within you is also the Spirit of truth.

THE SPIRIT OF TRUTH

Jesus calls him "the Spirit of truth" (John 14:17). There are two aspects to this idea. First, the Holy Spirit authored the Bible. In John 14:26, Jesus says that "the Helper, the Holy Spirit, whom the Father will send in my name, he will teach

---

5   Timothy Keller, "Who is the Spirit?" Sermon at Redeemer Presbyterian Church, New York, NY, July 4, 2010.

you all things and bring to your remembrance all that I have said to you." This is a promise specific to the apostles: the Holy Spirit, Jesus tells them, would guide them into all truth. It is because of this particular working of the Holy Spirit that Paul can call all of Scripture "God-breathed" (II Timothy 3:16-17).

In the same way, the Holy Spirit inspired Old Testament authors. "No prophecy was ever produced by the will of man," Peter writes of the Old Testament prophets, "but men spoke from God as they were carried along by the Holy Spirit" (II Peter 1:21).

This ought to challenge some of us who tend to equate the Holy Spirit with emotional experiences. Some think the primary indication of the Spirit's work is some dramatic moment of overwhelming emotion. But the most decisive work of the Spirit in all of history is his authorship of the Bible. The Spirit gave us the Scriptures.

If you really want to be filled with the Spirit of God, you will hang on his words. He has spoken to us by the prophets and the apostles and finally by his Son. You have the words of God the Spirit right there in your Bible. You have revelation from God to you. Are you hanging on his Word? Are you making time to read and study and think on the words of Scripture with other believers? Is the Bible the lens through which you view everything else in your life?

But the Holy Spirit did not just author the Bible. He also is the one who makes it real for you when you read it. The old theological term for this is *illumination*. For the Word of God to really sink into your life, you need the Holy Spirit to work. The apostle Paul put it this way: "now we have received not the spirit of the world, but the Spirit who is from God, that we might understand the things freely given us by God" (I Corinthians 2:12). God gives us his Spirit so we can understand his Word. If we were left to ourselves, this would be impossible.

This is a check to those of us who are brainiacs and theology wonks. The primary goal of Bible reading is not head knowledge, but a changed life. And you need the Holy Spirit for that to happen. All the natural intelligence in the world isn't going to do it. You may get a bigger brain, but it won't change your heart.

Jonathan Edwards wrote on this in a sermon in 1734 called "A Divine and Supernatural Light." Here is an excerpt:

> Thus there is a difference between having an *opinion*, that God is holy and gracious, and having a *sense* of the loveliness and beauty of that holiness and grace. There is a difference between having a rational judgment that honey is sweet, and having a sense of its sweetness. A man may have the former, that knows not how honey tastes; but a man cannot have the latter unless he has an idea of the taste of honey in his mind. So there is a difference between believing that a person is beautiful, and having a sense of his beauty. The former may be obtained by hearsay, but the latter only by seeing the countenance. There is a wide difference between mere speculative rational judging any thing to be excellent, and having a sense of its sweetness and beauty. The former

rests only in the head, speculation only is concerned in it; but the heart is concerned in the latter. When the heart is sensible of the beauty and amiableness of a thing, it necessarily feels pleasure in the apprehension. It is implied in a person's being heartily sensible of the loveliness of a thing, that the idea of it is sweet and pleasant to his soul; which is a far different thing from having a rational opinion that it is excellent.[6]

There is a difference between knowing that honey is sweet, and tasting the sweetness of honey. Similarly, there is a difference between knowing facts *about* God, and loving and delighting *in* God. The Holy Spirit is the one who takes head knowledge and makes it into heart knowledge. He is the one who takes the fact that God is good, and makes you "taste and see that the Lord is good" (Psalm 34:8). Because the Spirit who gives truth is also your great Helper.

THE SPIRIT IS THE HELPER

Jesus calls the Spirit "the Helper" (John 14:16). "Helper" is a tricky word to translate. Almost every translation renders it differently. Some say "Counselor," but are we supposed to think of a camp counselor? Some say "Comforter," but are we to think of a quilt we wrap up in on a cold winter's night? Even "Helper," which we prefer, makes the Spirit sound like someone who can give you a hand up.

Whenever you get that many translations for one word, it usually means there is not an adequate English word to really convey the meaning. The Greek word is *parakaleo*. *Para* means to stand alongside. Not in front, not behind, but to stand with you. *Kaleo* means to call, to prod, to urge on — even to argue with you. And so the picture Jesus is trying to give us of the Holy Spirit is not one of a spiritual masseuse intent upon taking you to the day spa. More like a field general, standing alongside you, urging you on to battle and victory.

In 1066 Norman armies under William the Conqueror successfully invaded England. The event was commemorated in the giant Bayeux Tapestry, a remarkably detailed record of the campaign. One of its scenes depicts a column of soldiers on horseback. They are followed by the bishop of Bayeux, who is busy poking the back row with a huge stick. The caption to this scene reads: "Bishop Odo *comforts* the soldiers."[7] That is the way the Spirit is a comforter and helper. He is urging you on to the life God has for you. He is prodding you, urging you, pushing you toward the mission of God.

The Holy Spirit spurs his people on to victory. One of his roles is to push you out into mission, so that you might proclaim the gospel in word and deed to the people around you. N.T. Wright says it this way: "The point of the Holy Spirit is to enable those who follow Jesus to take into all the world the news that he is

---

6 Jonathan Edwards, "A Divine and Supernatural Light." Sermon preached at Northampton, 1734 (http://www.monergism.com/thethreshold/articles/onsite/edwards_light.html).

7 The translation of the Latin in scene 54 of the tapestry: "*Hic Odo Eps (Episcopus) Baculu(m) Tenens Confortat Pueros.*"

Lord, that he has won the victory over the forces of evil, that a new world has opened up and that we are to help make it happen."[8]

Jesus sends the church into the world with a "great commission," to go and make disciples of all nations (Matthew 28:18-20). How are we going to do that? Can the church do that in its own strength? No way. It's impossible. The resistance is too tough, and we're fearful of opposition and persecution. Furthermore, we shoot ourselves in the foot by being hypocrites.

And yet even with all that, the gospel goes out and the Kingdom grows. Why? Because the Holy Spirit works in and through the church.

The Spirit is also working in you. He is putting people on your heart to pray for. He is bringing people across your path, convicting you of your need to be intentional in reaching out. The Spirit is pricking your conscience as you hear about injustices and hurting people, and the great needs in your city and around the world.

But it's not just mission. The Spirit also prods you toward holiness. It is the Holy Spirit that convicts us of sin (John 16:8). In a sense, it is when you become a Christian that things really start to get difficult. Rather than just their own voices and wills, Christians have the Spirit of God waging a battle against sin in their lives. The Spirit convicts of sin, and brings people to repentance. He does this in love, but sometimes it's the kind of love a friend might show to an addict or someone in a destructive lifestyle. You can almost come to blows in love. When the Holy Spirit convicts you, it is often a hard thing. Tim Keller says "sometimes he's against you, for you."[9]

The Spirit is also the one to pick you up off the mat when you fail. When you do wrong, it is so easy to think, "I've done it now. God is done with me." Satan wants to magnify those thoughts and feelings. But it's the Holy Spirit who prods you, who argues with you, until you remember who you are: a child of God. The Spirit reminds you of the world-changing truth of Romans 8:15-16: "You have received the Spirit of adoption as sons, by whom we cry, 'Abba! Father!' The Spirit himself bears witness with our spirit that we are children of God." When you sin and feel like you need to run away from God, it is the Spirit who comes in and says, "No, you are a child of God. This reality doesn't change just because you've failed."

"I believe in the Holy Spirit." This is no small confession. If you really believe in the Spirit, and give attention to his work in you, it will change your life.

Back to Rachel's shaky attempts to ride her bike on her own. We are all trying to figure out the balance, how to ride, how to reach out and demonstrate and declare the gospel in our community. The great comfort of this passage is that we are not left to do this on our own. Pray for the leaders in your church, that they might be instructed by the Holy Spirit, guided by the Holy Spirit, and held up by

8 N.T. Wright, *Simply Christian: Why Christianity Makes Sense* (New York, NY: HarperOne, 2006), 122.

9 Tim Keller, "Who Is the Spirit?"

the Holy Spirit as they lead your church body into mission and discipleship. And pray for evidence of the Spirit's work in your own life.

STUDY QUESTIONS:

- Are you trying to get to know the Spirit? Are you communing with him through prayer? Do you enter into his presence in worship and Bible reading? Are you asking him to work in your life and the life of your friends and your church?

- How can an awareness that the person of the Holy Spirit is dwelling within you impact your thoughts? Your behavior? In what specific ways?

- The Bible is the Word of God, directed by the Holy Spirit. Do you hang on his Word? Are you making time to read and study and think on the words of Scripture? Is the Bible the lens through which you view everything else in your life? Do you discuss and read it with other Christians and seek to understand it together?

- What does Tim Keller mean when he says of the Spirit, "sometimes he's against you, for you"? Why is the work of the Spirit that sanctifies us from sin so often challenging for us? What are some specific examples?

- How does knowing you are not alone change your mission to share the Kingdom in word and deed? What are some areas where you need to be encouraged to speak or act?

The Church

CHAPTER 10

¹I therefore, a prisoner for the Lord, urge you to walk in a manner worthy of the calling to which you have been called, ²with all humility and gentleness, with patience, bearing with one another in love, ³eager to maintain the unity of the Spirit in the bond of peace. ⁴There is one body and one Spirit — just as you were called to the one hope that belongs to your call — ⁵one Lord, one faith, one baptism, ⁶one God and Father of all, who is over all and through all and in all.

Ephesians 4:1-6

(Josh) like to play with Legos with my daughter. Our game is pretty simple: I build something; she tears it down. Only in recent months has she started to learn how to build. Tearing down came to her pretty naturally.

The same is true with us. We don't know who or what to build up, but we intuitively know how to tear down. It seems to be second nature.

The Apostles' Creed confesses belief in "the holy catholic church." The apostle Paul, in Ephesians 4, writes to encourage Christians to build up the church. Today, we are all called to that same mission, to build up the church. If we are going to fulfill this mission, we need to be aware of our natural tendencies to tear apart the things God makes. And so in this chapter, we will consider the ways in which we are tempted to tear apart Christ's church.

THE CENTRALITY OF THE CHURCH

We set ourselves on a path to wrecking the church when we fail to see its importance.

Human beings all need community. When Tuck Bartholomew was looking for an apartment in Philadelphia as he prepared to move there to plant City Church, his realtor asked him what kind of work he did. He shared that he was a minister. She said, "Given your kind of work, you must make a point of having dinner with your family." He thought this was kind of a strange statement, but said, "Well, yes, it is." The realtor, delighted and perhaps a bit amused, replied,

"How nostalgic!" He said it made him feel like he was Opie Taylor, and Aunt Bea was making pies in the other room. "How nostalgic!" This is how many people think about community in America. It is truly great and wonderful, but largely a memory from a bygone era.

But we still need and long for community. Our digital age hasn't changed that. All of the social networks in the world don't make up for our not having something to do on the weekend. We all know the benefits of being connected to a group of people. All of us know the sweetness of an embrace. We know how good it is to show up somewhere and know we belong, that people care about us. And we know the absence of this as well — the fear of being alone. The Bible tells us that we were made in the image of God, which means that we are hardwired as relational people. We were made to have lives that intersect with the lives of others.

We both pastor churches in urban neighborhoods where the search for community may be the single biggest "felt need." This is true for Christians and non-Christians alike. Though there are a lot of barriers to community in our world, we all have a hunger for it. Why else would coffee shops have become such a big deal in the last 20 years? Starbucks will tell you they are intentionally trying to be what sociologists call your "third place." You have home and work, but you need a third place to go and feel connected. That's why they write your name on the coffee cup. It feels good to walk in and have them call out, "Grande Pike Place, no room, for Josh!"

Bars are the same way. The most famous TV bar is Cheers, the place "where everybody knows your name." This feeling resonates with us, doesn't it? Bars exist for more than just alcohol — there are more efficient and inexpensive ways to get alcohol into your system than going to the bar. You can stop by the liquor store and get a buzz for a lot less money.[1] If it was simply about alcohol, everyone would do that. But there is more to it than that.

New City in Cincinnati used to meet on Sunday nights. My wife and I (Josh) would often go to a local pub to watch the end of the late football games. Without fail, there were always a few guys sitting at the bar, clearly alone, but striking up conversations with one another and the bartender. These guys could have been at home watching the game, but they wanted to be around other people. They wanted connection. They wanted community.

Bruce Larson and Keith Miller put it this way:

> What we really need is that special something that many people find in the local bar. The neighborhood bar is possibly the best counterfeit there is to the fellowship Christ wants to give his church. It's an imitation dispensing liquor instead of grace, escape rather than reality, but it is an accepting and inclusive fellowship. It is un-shockable. You can tell people secrets and they usually don't tell others or even want to. The bar flourishes, not because most people are alcoholics, but because

---

1   Or in New Orleans, the drive-through.

God has put in the human heart the desire to know and to be known, to love and to be loved. And so many seek a counterfeit at the price of a few beers.[2]

In his bestselling book, *Bowling Alone*, Harvard sociologist Robert Putnam argues from various studies that loss of community is connected to hurt and anger and shorter life spans. One of the most interesting charts Putnam employs shows that there is a correlation between social isolation and making obscene gestures towards others in traffic! The people who report the most community involvement and best relationships are more likely to give other drivers the benefit of the doubt. They are the least likely to get angry. Those who are least connected tend to flip people off the most![3] If you are prone to road rage, maybe you should get more involved in your church's community group!

Sometimes we feel like our need for community is a weakness. We think that we should be fine on our own. But in Genesis 2, God looks at Adam and says, "it is not good for man to be alone." It is crucial to note that God makes this statement *before* the fall, *before* sin has entered the world. A need for community is not a weakness; it is simply how you were made. God himself has community within the Trinity, and we are made in his image.

Simply surrounding ourselves with people is not enough. We need the community of the church. When Paul begins this section of Ephesians 4, he says, "I therefore, a prisoner for the Lord, urge you to walk in a manner worthy of the calling to which you have been called" (Ephesians 4:1). First, Paul calls attention to the fact that he is a prisoner. He reminds the Ephesians that the life of the church is so important that he's willing to sit in jail awaiting death for it. Paul uses this capital to call them to live out their calling in the context of the church. Paul, who has risked his life, is now telling them how to do church life together.

The second thing to notice about verse 1 is that this is the pivot point of Paul's letter to the Ephesians. The first three chapters of Ephesians are all about doctrine. In particular, Paul is telling the Ephesians what God has done for them in Jesus. Before Jesus, you were alienated from God, and alienated from one another. But now, if you believe in Jesus, you are reconciled to God and to one another. You are part of God's family.

Now, in chapter 4, Paul begins to apply the doctrine he's just imparted. He tells the Ephesians to "walk in a manner worthy of your calling." Be who God has called you to be. And, practically, what does that mean? You are to live in peace and love and unity in the church. This is the first thing he mentions: before he gets to family, before he gets to evangelism, before he gets to spiritual warfare. The theater for living out the life God has for you is in the church.

The church is not an afterthought to Paul. We tend to believe that the chief interest of the Christian life is our being saved in Christ, and that being

2 Bruce Larson and Keith Miller, *The Edge of Adventure* (Waco, TX: Word Books, 1983), 156.
3 Robert Putnam, *Bowling Alone: The Collapse and Revival of American Community* (New York, NY: Simon & Schuster, 2001), 233.

connected to a church is of minor importance. But Paul assumes that if you're a Christian, you'll begin to work out your Christianity by doing life together with other believers in the church.

The church is fundamental to living out your identity in Christ. Think about the way the church is described in the Bible.

- *The church is Christ's bride* (Ephesians 5:25-32). How much does Christ love the church? Like a husband loves his wife.
- *The church is God's family.* "So then you are no longer strangers and aliens, but you are fellow citizens with the saints and members of the household of God" (Ephesians 1:19). God is not just saving individuals, but he is making a people for himself.
- *The church is a magnificent temple.* "You yourselves like living stones are being built up as a spiritual house" (I Peter 2:5).[4]
- *The church is Christ's body.* "And he put all things under his feet and gave him as head over all things to the church, which is his body, the fullness of him who fills all in all" (Ephesians 1:22-23). The church is so close to the heart of God, so central to his work in the world, that he calls us the *body* of Christ. As we express our union with him through service, worship, and love, the church becomes the physical manifestation of our Savior on the earth.

It's easy to rip on the church, with its warts, flaws, and quirks. And, quite honestly, we have zero interest in defending everything about the church. Despite its problems, though, you cannot give up on the church. Jesus is the only person who has the right to give up on it, and he hasn't. He still works at beautifying his bride.

Nashville artist Derek Webb, writing from the perspective of Jesus, sings, "you cannot care for me with no regard for her / if you love me you will love the church."[5] John Stott puts it this way:

> On earth she is often in rags and tatters, stained and ugly, despised and persecuted. But one day she will be seen for what she is, nothing less than the bride of Christ, "free from spots, wrinkles, or another disfigurement," holy and without blemish, beautiful and glorious. It is to this constructive end that Christ has been working and is continuing to work. The bride does not make herself presentable; it is the bridegroom who labors to beautify her in order to present her to himself.[6]

As pastors we have tried to combat low views of the church by emphasizing the importance of membership. The Bible teaches that Christianity isn't just about you and Jesus; it's about living out your faith in the context of the covenant community. Most of the New Testament is composed of letters written to specific churches. When the apostles did evangelism, they didn't just say to

4 Also see Ephesians 2:20-22.
5 Derek Webb, "The Church." *She Must and Shall Go Free* (INO Records, 2003).
6 John R.W. Stott, *The Message of Ephesians* (Downers Grove, IL: InterVarsity Press, 1986).

individuals, "Great, you're saved. Read your Bible." They set up churches in every town they went to, and they appointed elders to help lead. The Bible makes the church central to the Christian life.

It's time to stop dating the church.[7] Marry her. Jump into a church community. Find a place where you can serve, where you are most needed, where you can worship and do life with other Christians.

Consider these challenging words from Charles Spurgeon:

> I know there are some who say, "well, I have given myself to the Lord, but I do not intend to give myself to the church." Now why not? "Because I can be a Christian without it."
>
> Are you quite clear about that? You can be as good a Christian by disobedience to your Lord's commands as by being obedient?
>
> What is a brick made for? To help build a house. It is of no use for that brick to tell you that it is just as good a brick while it is kicking about on the ground as it would be in the house. It is a good-for-nothing brick.
>
> So you, rolling-stone Christians, I do not believe you are answering your purpose. You are living contrary to the life which Christ would have you live, and you are much to blame for the injury you do.[8]

If the church is not important to you, you won't make it a priority, and you won't get involved. But this hurts the church, because it misses out on you and your gifts. It cannot be all that God has called it to be — it can never improve — unless his people are fully engaged with it. You need the church, and the church needs you. And it specifically needs you to work for its unity.

THE UNITY OF THE CHURCH

Paul goes on to say that we should be "*eager* to maintain the unity of the Spirit" (Ephesians 4:3). We all know there is a difference between begrudgingly doing something, and eagerly doing something. If you have kids, you know. You want your kids not just to obey when you ask them to do something. You want them to be quick to respond, and to do it without grumbling and complaining. The same is true if you manage anyone in your workplace. It's one thing for people to follow your direction while whining and complaining, and it's another thing altogether to have an employee who is eager to respond.

Paul uses such strong language here because he knows our default setting is to not live this way. We are destructive to the church when we fail to see its critical importance, but also when we fail to seek its unity. Like my daughter with the Legos, it's easier to tear down than to build up. Paul says that you should not only pursue the unity of the church, but that you should be *eager* to do it. Some translations say "make every effort." This is such a big deal that you need to go

---

7 Joshua Harris has written a popular book on the church called *Stop Dating the Church* (Sisters, OR: Multnomah, 2004).

8 Spurgeon, quoted in Harris, *Stop Dating the Church*, 45-46.

"over and above" to make this happen. Don't drag your feet. Jump at the chance to be a peacemaker and pursue unity in the church.

In verses 4-6, Paul says you can do this. It sounds hard, because people are difficult, but you can do it. You can do it because God has already made you one with the church. He has already purchased unity in the church with the blood of Christ. "But now in Christ Jesus you who once were far off have been brought near by the blood of Christ. For he himself is our peace, who has made us both one and has broken down in his flesh the dividing wall of hostility..." (Ephesians 2:13-14).

This is why Paul writes so passionately about oneness in chapter 4. "There is one body and one Spirit — just as you were called to the one hope that belongs to your call — one Lord, one faith, one baptism, one God and Father of all, who is over all and through all and in all" (Ephesians 4:4-6). God has already made you one. He has reconciled you to one another. Now you just need to live out that unity. It's like a coach who says, "Whether you like it or not, you guys are teammates. Now, go and play like it."

What is the basis for unity in the church? That we like each other? That we're exactly alike? That we always agree? No, the basis for unity is what God has done to reconcile us to one another. This is one reason why worship services have historically had a "Passing of the Peace" as one of the elements; it's not just a chance to say hello to neighbors. In both of our churches, the Passing of the Peace usually follows the Prayer of Confession and Assurance of Pardon because it reminds us that Christ reconciled people not just to God, but to one another.

How do we achieve this unity? "Walk in a manner worthy of the calling to which you have been called..." And what does that walk look like? "[W]ith all humility and gentleness, with patience, bearing with one another in love" (Ephesians 4:1-2). The word for humility here in verse 2 literally means "lowliness." This was not considered a virtue in the Greco-Roman world. Not until Jesus Christ was humility proclaimed as a virtue rather than a weakness. The gospel message scandalized the pagan world when it claimed that the God of the universe came down from heaven and humbled himself, taking the form of a servant.[9]

Humility is the key to unity because pride, its opposite, is behind every single division we see. C.S. Lewis called pride "the Great Sin." It causes you to be defensive and makes you bitter. We become competitive, overly concerned with being noticed, and we feel so slighted by those around us that we become unable to forgive. Pride encourages you to feel better by tearing someone else down.

But humility makes you low. And it makes it okay to be there, because that's where Jesus is. When you're not pursuing a name for yourself, you are free to glorify God and serve other people. When your fame isn't the point, you can give credit to others. When your worth isn't attached to people's perception of you, you can freely admit when you're wrong. When winning the argument and

---

9 See Philippians 2; Matthew 11:29.

proving your intelligence isn't the goal, you can listen, truly listen, to the person sitting across from you.

If humility is the disposition, then gentleness is the demeanor. Gentleness flows from a humble heart and a humble spirit. When you know you're not great, you're not so severe when you see the faults of others.

Paul also mentions "patience and forbearance in love." This is how you know Paul is not an ivory tower guy. He has been a pastor and a church planter. He works with people. And so he says, in order to preserve unity, you will need to endure. You will need to be patient. The word "patient" means "long-suffering." Note that "suffering" is a part of that word.

Do you know the best way to wreck a church? Go in with the expectation that everyone will do everything right, no one will hurt you, no one will step on your toes. Believe that the worship will always be to your liking and that everyone will always be friendly. You will be terribly disappointed, and grow bitter.

Paul encourages us to have patience and forbearance, because, just like you, everyone in the church is a sinner. We hurt each other. But patience and long-suffering keep you coming back. Patience extends grace, puts up with wrongs, believes the best. It overlooks mistakes. You are called to this as a Christian because this is how God has acted toward you. How is God's character described most often in the Old Testament? "Slow to anger, abounding in love."[10]

Have you made sense of the fact yet that Jesus died for you when were a sinner?[11] Jesus died for you when you had bad ideas. He cared for you when you did bad things. To the degree that we know and believe Jesus has been humble and gentle and patient and long-suffering toward us, to that degree these qualities will begin to be manifest in our interactions with other people. You will long for, love, and nurture the unity of the church. And a love for the church's unity will lead to a love for its catholicity.

THE CATHOLICITY OF THE CHURCH

You can wreck the church by not seeing its importance, by not pursuing its unity, and also by not recognizing its catholicity. The Apostles' Creed says, "I believe in one holy catholic church." Many people think this refers to the Roman Catholic Church, but the Greek word *katholikos* means "universal." In saying the church is catholic, we are affirming that the church's message is valid and relevant to every age in every situation and in every culture. And this church exists wherever the gospel is preached and the sacraments are given, wherever mission is happening to neighbors. Wherever Jesus Christ is lifted up as Lord, there is the catholic church.

---

10 Exodus 34:6, Numbers 14:18, Nehemiah 9:17, Psalm 86:15, 103:8, 145:8, Joel 2:13, Jonah 4:2.
11 Romans 5:8.

But we often don't see it that way, do we? Maybe you've heard the old Emo Phillips story:

> I was walking across a bridge one day, and I saw a man standing on the edge, about to jump off. So I ran over and said, "stop! Don't do it!"
> "Why shouldn't I?" he said.
> I said, "Well, there's so much to live for."
> He said, "Like what?"
> I said, "Well...are you religious or atheist?"
> He said, "Religious." I said, "Me too! Are you Christian or Buddhist?"
> He said, "Christian." I said, "Me too! Are you Catholic or Protestant?"
> He said, "Protestant." I said, "Me too! What kind?"
> He said, "Baptist." I said, "Wow! Me too! What franchise?"
> He said, "Baptist Church of God." I said, "Me too! Are you original Baptist Church of God, or are you Reformed Baptist Church of God?"
> He said, "Reformed Baptist Church of God." I said, "Me too! Are you Reformed Baptist Church of God, Confession of 1879, or Reformed Baptist Church of God, Confession of 1915?"
> He said, "Reformed Baptist Church of God, Confession of 1915." I said, "Die, heretic scum!" and pushed him off the bridge.[12]

You can wreck the church by wrecking an individual congregation, but you can also hurt the church's work and witness when you have a bad attitude toward other churches and denominations. The call to catholicity is the call to stop picking on each other. After all, as Paul says in Ephesians 4, we have the same God and Father.

This is not a call for ignoring differences. A major weakness of the modern ecumenical movement has been to try and boil everything down to the lowest common denominator. That is not what Paul is urging us to in pursuing unity. But he is calling for us to have humility and gentleness and love and patience with other Christians. We are to lay aside less important differences when possible. He is calling us to look for and celebrate what we have in common.

We may have to argue and debate, and sometimes even fight, but we need to do it the right way. This is one reason why the Apostles' Creed is so important. It outlines for us the core doctrines of Christianity. Those who fall inside it can still have differences and even fight from time to time, but they can fight like brothers.

My three brothers and I (Josh) fought a lot growing up. But the way I fought with my brothers is completely different than the way I'd fight with someone breaking into my house. We all need to understand the difference.

Paul tells us in other places that there are wolves, and the church needs to be defended against them. But when taking aim, make sure you shoot at the wolf. All too often Christians aim indiscriminately, and they may get the wolf, but they hit a lot of sheep in the process.

---

12 Paraphrased from "The Wisdom of Emo Phillips" (http://cmgm.stanford.edu/-lkozar/EmoPhillips.html).

The call to recognize the church's catholicity is a call to watch how we talk about other churches. We ought to believe the best, and not slander or cast other churches in a bad light. We should regularly pray for (and root for) other churches in our cities. The kingdom is bigger than any one congregation. And if you need to leave your church to go to another one, do so without feeling the need to air your grievances on the way out.

But most of all, the call to catholicity is a call to partnering in the work of the gospel. Individual congregations and denominations would do well to recognize they are not on mission alone. The resources and witness of the church are so much stronger when congregations work together to love their cities and embody the gospel.

Most of us don't want to wreck the church; it's just our default manner. Like my daughter with the Legos, tearing down is easier than building up. The Creed calls us to build up the church and to pursue its unity and peace.

STUDY QUESTIONS:

- Do you have a community deficit in your life?

- Why is humility so important for unity? Where is it hardest for you to lay aside your pride?

- Should we be choosing which church to attend based on what programs it can provide us, or based on where we are most needed?

- If our unity in the church is eternal, why do you think we have such a hard time experiencing and enjoying this unity?

- What specific things can you do to build up the unity of your local church today? What pet concerns or felt needs should you lay aside for the sake of building up the unity of your church?

- Are you encouraging your church to pursue catholicity in the ways it interacts with other churches and denominations?

The Forgiveness of Sins

CHAPTER 11

²⁶Now as they were eating, Jesus took bread, and after blessing it broke it and gave it to the disciples, and said, "take, eat; this is my body." ²⁷And he took a cup, and when he had given thanks he gave it to them, saying, "drink of it, all of you, ²⁸for this is my blood of the covenant, which is poured out for many for the forgiveness of sins. ²⁹I tell you I will not drink again of this fruit of the vine until that day when I drink it new with you in my Father's kingdom."

Matthew 26:26-29

In talking about the Christian faith to other people, there is a strong chance you are going to be misunderstood. When Christians talk about salvation, or having assurance of their salvation, people can be put off. Because very often they assume that what you are saying is, "I've got it all together. I'm righteous. I'm holy." Or even worse, "I'm better than you."

Now Christians haven't always done a good job of defusing that misconception. Too often we come across just that way: self-righteous, judgmental, thinking we've got it all together.

But even if you do everything right, even if you're humble, compassionate, selfless, and gentle, you will still at times be misunderstood. Our whole culture is built on the notion that we get what we earn. And our pop culture teaches us that heaven is the exclusive reward of "good" people. So if you say you know you are going to heaven, it's just assumed that you're arrogant, that you think you've earned your place in heaven.

But that's not what Christianity teaches about heaven or salvation. The Apostles' Creed reminds us of this when it states, "I believe in the forgiveness of sins." If you are a Christian, what is your hope? That your good outweighs your bad? That you are better than the woman sitting next to you? No, the Creed reminds us that our true hope, our only hope, is that Jesus has made it possible for our sins to be forgiven.

Matthew 26 gives an account of the Last Supper, so named because it takes place the night before Jesus died. But in another way, it's actually the First

Supper, the first of many suppers that Christians celebrate. Christians all over the globe and throughout the centuries celebrate the Lord's Supper as a part of their worship. In the Supper, Jesus teaches us something about the meaning of his death and why this is the ground for all Christian hope.

THE BREAD

The bread in the Supper tells us about the significance of his death. To see this, you need to understand the backdrop of the meal that Jesus is sitting down to eat with his disciples. If we back up a bit to Matthew 26:19, we know this isn't just any meal. They are celebrating the Passover. Some of you know about Passover because you're Jewish, or you have some family or friends who are.

The Passover is a meal that started in ancient Israel. The purpose of the meal was to recount and celebrate Israel's deliverance from Egypt. It was a perpetual meal, meaning you were supposed to do it again and again. "This day shall be for you a memorial day, and you shall keep it as a feast to the Lord; throughout your generations, as a statute forever, you shall keep it as a feast" (Exodus 12:14).

Verse 26 tells us that Jesus acts as the presider over the meal. He breaks the bread and blesses it. Typically, the presider would then say something like this: "this is the bread of affliction which our fathers ate in the land of Egypt." In other words, as we eat this bread we remember the suffering of our ancestors. We eat unleavened bread to remind us that they left Egypt in such haste there wasn't time for the bread to rise. They suffered as they did so that we would be delivered.

Jesus blesses the bread according to tradition, and he breaks and distributes it like any Passover presider would. But then Jesus breaks from the traditional formula. He says, "This is my body." In other words, this is the bread of my affliction. Jesus is saying, "I am going to suffer so that you can be delivered."

The exodus was the defining event in the Jewish community. It was a picture of God's salvation and love for his people. God rescued them. He saved them. The Jews always looked to the exodus as proof of his love. But now Jesus says there is an even greater event, an even greater liberation. The first Passover was eaten the night before the people were liberated from their slavery in Egypt. Now Jesus is eating this meal the night before another liberation. He is not freeing them from Pharaoh, but from slavery to sin and death.

Jesus is making a tremendous statement here. He is saying that his death is now the definitive event in the history of the world. It will be the proof of God's love, the ultimate means of liberation. His death is the way to victory. There is nothing bigger, nothing more central, nothing more important to your health and happiness and wholeness than the death of Jesus. It is the most important thing that has ever happened.

This is why Paul and the other Christian leaders and missionaries would later say, "I decided to know nothing among you except Jesus Christ and him crucified" (I Corinthians 2:2). It is not one truth among others. It is *the* truth, *the* thing, *the* definitive event.

This is important because every other religion and philosophy tells us that it's what *you* do that is most important. But not the Christian faith. The Bible tells us it is what Jesus has done that is definitive. Jesus is the Liberator. He's the Savior. He's the one who can free you from slavery to sin and death. Heaven, salvation, and liberation don't arise from what we can do for God, but from what he has done for us in Jesus. "This is the bread of my affliction. I've come to suffer for you."

THE CUP

While bread tells us about the significance of Jesus' death, the cup tells us what his death accomplishes. Again, we have to explore a little background to understand the full weight of Jesus' explanation. "And he took a cup, and when he had given thanks he gave it to them, saying, 'Drink of it, all of you, for this is my blood of the covenant, which is poured out for many for the forgiveness of sins'" (Matthew 26:27-28).

This is pretty strange when you think about it. Jesus refers to his blood, and a cup, and drinking it. It's fairly gory. Unless you are a fan of teenage vampire novels, it could gross you out. In fact, all this talk of blood sacrifice is a stumbling block to many people.

But Jesus isn't the first one to talk about the necessity of the shedding of blood for the forgiveness of sins. Blood and blood sacrifice are everywhere in the Bible, especially in the Old Testament. Referring to the Old Testament, the writer of Hebrews says, "Indeed, under the law almost everything is purified with blood" (Hebrews 9:22). The Old Testament sacrificial system called for regular sacrifices by priests, where the blood of animals was shed on behalf of the people for the forgiveness of sins.

The concept of sacrifice to satisfy a requirement made by God seems horribly primitive and dark. Do we really need a religion like this? Don't we need a religion that inspires love and morality? The shedding of blood brings up all the opposite associations. Violence, murder, war — these are not exactly positive, life-affirming images. Sometimes the Christian faith has been mockingly called the "slaughterhouse religion." Why were these blood sacrifices so important in the Old Testament? It is not as strange as you think, when you consider what a powerful symbol blood was in the ancient world.[1]

---

1   We are indebted to Rev. Matt Brown, pastor of Resurrection Presbyterian Church in Brooklyn. His preaching on Hebrews helped us to understand the logic and importance of blood sacrifice.

Blood Tells Us Something Is Broken

First, blood indicates something was broken. Something had gone wrong. This is not too difficult to understand. If blood begins to gush from you, you know something is not good. Without blood, we dry up. We return to dust. So blood sacrifices were meant to show people that what is wrong with us is serious business. If the spilling of blood indicates something is wrong, then a blood offering shows us the severity of our crimes against God.

Blood Is Associated With Guilt

Second, blood carried connotations of guilt in the ancient world. We still use expressions that reflect this: "there is blood on your hands," or "blood on your head." Blood offerings demonstrate that we are complicit, that we ourselves are guilty. We are not innocent bystanders in a world gone wrong, but we contribute to what is wrong with the world. This is what the people of Israel were affirming when they came with their sacrifices.

We all know something about guilt. Sir Arthur Conan Doyle, author of the Sherlock Holmes series, was known for his practical jokes. Apparently he took great pleasure in teasing his friends, especially some who were a little rough around the edges. One day he sent an unsigned telegram to each of his closest friends that simply said, "All is discovered. Flee at once." Most immediately left town in a rush![2]

We all have a guilty conscience to one degree or another. Every one of us is familiar with guilt and shame. We all know somewhere deep down, the problems in the world aren't all *out there*. Some of the problems reside *in us*. That is why we spend so much time covering things up, not letting people in. We don't want to be found out for who we are. We don't want people to know the thoughts that cross our mind, the selfishness in our heart, the things we've done.

Blood Stains

Third, blood's ability to stain made it a powerful symbol. This makes sense to us too. Blood is hard to get out. In the ancient world, it was also considered a contaminant; it made people unclean. Blood offerings tell us that we are stained by sin. The stain on our conscience is not easily removed. We know we have failed. We are complicit. And we just cannot shake that sense.

All of this is in the background of Jesus' words here in Matthew 26. "Drink of it, all of you, for this is my blood of the covenant, which is poured out for the many for the forgiveness of sins." Jesus is telling us that his blood is what will save us.

He even hints at how this happens. Notice he says that his blood is poured out "for many." This is the language of substitution. The Greek preposition means something like "on behalf of," "instead of." Jesus' blood is poured out instead of yours.

2 "Men Met in Hotel Lobbies," *Washington Post* (June 16, 1901), 18.

BUT NO LAMB?

Think again about the Passover meal. There is bread. There is the cup — four cups actually, representing the great promises of deliverance made by God in Exodus 6. But the main course in the Passover is the lamb.

God delivers the people from Egypt by sending a series of plagues on the Egyptians. The last plague, the one that finally convinces Pharaoh to free the Hebrews, sends the Angel of Judgment to pass over the land. He strikes down the firstborn in every family and they fall dead. But the Hebrews were told to have a feast on the night before and to slay a lamb. They were to smear the lamb's blood over their doorposts so that the judgment of God would pass them over. This is where the name Passover comes from.

The only way to be saved was to take shelter under the blood. You would either have a dead lamb, or a dead son. But God's judgment was coming.

Isn't it interesting here in Matthew 26, that the lamb is never mentioned? It was like no other Passover meal ever celebrated before. And for Christians who celebrate the Lord's Supper, why don't we have a lamb every time we do this? The answer is in the blood of Jesus. John the Baptist saw Jesus coming toward him one day, and said, "behold, the Lamb of God, who takes away the sin of the world" (John 1:29). Jesus is the sacrificial Lamb.

Hebrews 9:22 says that "without the shedding of blood there is no forgiveness of sins." When Jesus tells the disciples, "My blood is going to be poured out for the forgiveness of sins," he is telling them he will be slain so they don't have to be.

The forgiveness of sins comes only through the blood of Jesus. Blood tells us that our sin is serious — so serious that it takes the death of the Son of God to bring about forgiveness. It is Jesus' blood that reconciles us to God. This is why it is called the blood of the covenant. It represents the reconciliation of God and his people. Blood stains, but Jesus' blood washes away the stain of sin, so much so that the Bible can describe forgiven sinners as "white as snow." Jesus promises them they will drink with him from the fruit of the vine "in my Father's kingdom" (Matthew 26:29). "This is my blood of the covenant, which is poured out for the forgiveness of sins."

YOUR RESPONSE

How should you respond to this? If you believe it to be true, you must respond. Jesus' death is the most definitive event in history. When the Creed confesses belief in "the communion of saints and the forgiveness of sins," it is a call to action.

Take Jesus In

First, we're called to take Jesus in. Jesus says this himself. "Take, eat... drink of it, all of you." You have to make this yours. The Lord's Supper is a picture of what it means to believe in Jesus. When you come to any meal, you can sit at the table and look at the bread, and look at the wine, but unless you're eating, it doesn't do you any good. The same is true with Jesus. You need to make the benefits of the cross yours by taking him in.

If you're not a believer, or you're not sure if you've really taken him into your life, then now is the time. Take him in by faith. Trust in him for the forgiveness of your sins. Admit that you've rebelled against God and that you need a Savior, and believe his blood is sufficient to cleanse you.

Celebrate Often

Second, we are called to celebrate the Lord's Supper often. It doesn't say it here in Matthew, but when Paul writes about the Lord's Supper elsewhere in the New Testament, he says, "For as often as you eat this bread and drink the cup, you proclaim the Lord's death until he comes" (II Corinthians 11:26). Paul emphasizes the frequency with which we should celebrate the Lord's Supper. In other words, it's not just something you partake of once. You should do it regularly.

The Lord's Supper should be celebrated often because it puts the death of Jesus in the center of your mind. It reminds you of the significance of the cross of Christ. The old theologians said that the Lord's Supper is one of the "means of grace." The means of grace are the things you absolutely need in order to grow in your faith, to see God begin to take over and transform your life. Most of us easily see how the Bible, or prayer, or gathering with other Christians are means of grace, but all of the old theologians list the Lord's Supper, too. You need it in order to grow and live out the life God has for you.

In the last book of *The Lord of the Rings*, Pippin (one of the main characters) is standing at the gate of the fortress. The gate has been destroyed, the walls have been breached, and the demon king is about to come in and destroy all the people inside the city. Just as it looks like they are done for, Pippin hears a horn in the distance. The King of Rohan comes, and he rides to his death, but in doing so he saves the city.

From then on, every time Pippin hears a horn blowing in the distance, he bursts into tears. The sound of the horn was a tangible reminder of his salvation. Going through life, he knew that he was alive because the king had come and died for him. He knew this all the time, but when the horn blew, he knew it in a deeper way.[3]

The Lord's Supper is your horn blowing in the distance. The Lord's Supper helps you know the significance of Christ's death in a deeper way.

The Table Can Change You

Are you struggling with insecurity? The Table should give you confidence. Do you know how valuable you are? So valuable that Jesus allowed his body to be broken, his blood to be spilt. He wants you to dine with him!

Are you proud, arrogant, judgmental? The Table should make you humble. On your own, you are so lost that nothing less than the blood of Jesus could save

---

3 I (Josh) think I first heard Tim Keller use this illustration, but I've heard others use it since.

you. There is no room for pride at the Lord's Table, not if you really see what is happening. How can you feel superior to anyone else when you're reminded of the depth of your sin?

Are you suffering? Come to the Table for comfort. He knows. As one pastor says, "This is the only God with scars." He has been there. And he is with you now in the middle of whatever you're dealing with.

Are you selfish? Apathetic? When you come to the Lord's Supper, it transforms you. You can't keep living the same way anymore, because your life was bought at a price.

This reminds us of Ernest Gordon. I (Ray) met Gordon when he was the retired chaplain of Princeton University.[4] He had been a prisoner of war in a Japanese prison camp in Thailand many years earlier. Gordon wrote a book about his experiences called *Through the Valley of the Kwai*. One day, the prisoners were out in the valley working…

> The day's work had ended; the tools were being counted. When the party was about to be dismissed the Japanese guard declared that a shovel was missing. He strode up and down in front of the men, ranting and denouncing them for their wickedness, their stupidity…
>
> Screaming in broken English, he demanded that the guilty one step forward to take his punishment. No one moved. The guard's rage reached new heights of violence.
>
> "All die! All die!" he shrieked.
>
> To show that he meant what he said, [he cocked the rifle], put it to his shoulder, and looked down the sights, ready to fire at the first man he saw at the end of them [and then on down the line].
>
> At that moment [a man from the Argyll regiment] stepped forward, stood stiffly to attention, and said calmly, "I did it."
>
> The guard unleashed all his whipped-up hatred; he kicked the hapless prisoner and beat him with his fists. Still the Argyll stood rigidly at attention. The blood was streaming down his face, but he made no sound. His silence goaded the guard to an excess of rage. He seized his rifle by the barrel and lifted it high over his head. With a final howl he brought the butt down on the skull of the Argyll, who sank limply to the ground and did not move. Although it was perfectly evident that he was dead, the guard continued to beat him and stopped only when exhausted.
>
> The men of the work detail picked up their comrade's body, shouldered their tools, and marched back to camp. When the tools were counted again at the guardhouse, no shovel was missing.[5]

He died for them. He was innocent — the shovel wasn't even missing. But he knew that if he didn't step forward then they all were going to die. His blood was shed to save them. And he didn't just save them physically. Those men

---

4 I met with Gordon several times in 1992 when I was a student in Princeton.
5 Ernest Gordon, *Through the Valley of the Kwai* (New York, NY: Wipf & Stock, 1997), 104-105.

would never be the same. They would never live as selfishly as they would have otherwise.

It is a powerful moment, even for us so many years later. It humbles us, and almost makes us want to live our lives differently — and we didn't even know the guy. He didn't die for our sake.

But in Christ, we have a loving, compassionate Savior, one who knows the depths of our sin, the deepest, most tragic and confusing parts of us, our rebellious hearts and wills, and who still chooses to give his life for us. The Lord's Supper is our constant reminder of the depths of his love and understanding. And as you reflect on that, and come to the Table, it changes you; it makes you more like him.

STUDY QUESTIONS:

- If you are a Christian, what is your hope? That your good outweighs your bad? That you are better than the person next to you? On what basis do you hope?

- Why do you think that most churches in history have celebrated communion every time they worshipped? Do you believe that it is only a ritual?

- How does the gospel allow you to forgive others who have hurt you? Who in your life do you need to forgive today?

- What steps can you take to make your celebration of the Lord's Supper more meaningful?

The Resurrection of the Body

CHAPTER 12

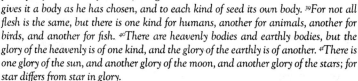

35But someone will ask, "how are the dead raised? With what kind of body do they come?" 36You foolish person! What you sow does not come to life unless it dies. 37And what you sow is not the body that is to be, but a bare kernel, perhaps of wheat or of some other grain. 38But God gives it a body as he has chosen, and to each kind of seed its own body. 39For not all flesh is the same, but there is one kind for humans, another for animals, another for birds, and another for fish. 40There are heavenly bodies and earthly bodies, but the glory of the heavenly is of one kind, and the glory of the earthly is of another. 41There is one glory of the sun, and another glory of the moon, and another glory of the stars; for star differs from star in glory.

42So is it with the resurrection of the dead. What is sown is perishable; what is raised is imperishable. 43It is sown in dishonor; it is raised in glory. It is sown in weakness; it is raised in power. 44It is sown a natural body; it is raised a spiritual body. If there is a natural body, there is also a spiritual body. 45Thus it is written, "the first man Adam became a living being"; the last Adam became a life-giving spirit. 46But it is not the spiritual that is first but the natural, and then the spiritual. 47The first man was from the earth, a man of dust; the second man is from heaven. 48As was the man of dust, so also are those who are of the dust, and as is the man of heaven, so also are those who are of heaven. 49Just as we have borne the image of the man of dust, we shall also bear the image of the man of heaven.

50I tell you this, brothers: flesh and blood cannot inherit the kingdom of God, nor does the perishable inherit the imperishable. 51Behold! I tell you a mystery. We shall not all sleep, but we shall all be changed, 52in a moment, in the twinkling of an eye, at the last trumpet. For the trumpet will sound, and the dead will be raised imperishable, and we shall be changed. 53For this perishable body must put on the imperishable, and this mortal body must put on immortality. 54When the perishable puts on the imperishable, and the mortal puts on immortality, then shall come to pass the saying that is written:

"Death is swallowed up in victory."

55"O death, where is your victory?

O death, where is your sting?"

56The sting of death is sin, and the power of sin is the law. 57But thanks be to God, who gives us the victory through our Lord Jesus Christ.

58Therefore, my beloved brothers, be steadfast, immovable, always abounding in the work of the Lord, knowing that in the Lord your labor is not in vain.

I Corinthians 15:35-58

If you are ever tempted to think of doctrine as merely an academic concern, you simply have to come to the last two clauses of the Apostles' Creed to remember how practical theology can be. "I believe in the resurrection of the body, and the life everlasting." Can anything be more relevant? We all think about the fundamental human questions of death and what happens after we die. We will deal with the life everlasting in the final chapter, but here we'll consider what the Apostles' Creed means when it confesses belief in the resurrection of the body.

THE RESURRECTION OF THE DEAD AND YOUR HOPE

The Christian faith tells us something that, if true, is really glorious. Namely, that death has been conquered and we need not fear it any longer.

Our Hope is Resurrected Bodies, Not Immortal Souls

Most pop-cultural ideas of heaven or the afterlife have to do with the immortality of the soul. Your body may die, but your soul lives on. In some ways, this reflects ancient Greco-Roman culture. The body was the tomb of the soul, and death simply freed your soul from the body.

It is important that you know that this is not the Creed's view, nor is it the Biblical view. Very simply, the Bible teaches that when Christ returns at the end of time, there will be a resurrection of the dead. As Christians, we don't believe that our eternal destiny is to be disembodied souls united to God. There will be a physicality to the afterlife and we will have resurrected bodies.

Yes, there is an "intermediate state," as theologians call the time between our death and Jesus' returning at Judgment Day to usher in the resurrection of our bodies. During that in-between time, most Christians believe that souls will live without bodies. But the Apostles' Creed expresses what the Bible emphasizes — the Christian hope is for the resurrection of the body for eternity.

The Old Testament hints at this. Fifteen hundred years before Christ, Job said, "After my skin has been destroyed, yet in my flesh I shall see God, whom I shall see for myself, and my eyes shall behold..." (Job 19:26-27). This theme continues and expands in the New Testament.

So when Paul learns that many in this church plant at Corinth are teaching that there is no resurrection of the body, he is alarmed. For Paul, this is no minor point. He says earlier in I Corinthians 15 that if you don't believe in the resurrection of our bodies, then you don't believe in the resurrection of Jesus. The two are connected. This is why Paul calls Jesus' resurrection the "first fruits" in a harvest of all God's people.[1] The resurrection of Jesus is just the beginning. At the end, there will be a general resurrection.

---

1   I Corinthians 15:20-24.

What will our resurrection bodies be like? We don't know a lot, but we do know they will be the product of a radical transformation, with both continuity and discontinuity from our current experience. Our bodies will be like they are now, and yet also different and more glorious.

In verses 37-41, Paul uses the analogy of a seed and a mature plant. Here we see both continuity and discontinuity. The seed contains the whole plant, and yet looks very different. Thus Paul says that your new body will be "you" (the dead will be raised, verse 52), but he also says you will be changed (verse 51). This he rightly labels a mystery.

Think of the resurrection appearances of Jesus. At first the disciples did not even recognize him; something was different. And yet when he broke bread with them, they recognized him. It was really him. He had the wounds of the cross to prove it.

The theological term for this is "glorification." When theologians use this term, what they mean to say is that God has simply completed what he has already begun in you. If you are a follower of Christ, and have been brought to faith in him, then God has begun a work in you. He's forgiven your sins. He's washed your guilt clean. In a very real way, you're a "new creation" in Christ. He is already sanctifying and transforming you. But it is only at the resurrection of the dead that this work will be completed. Further, glorification will be not just of your soul, but of your body as well.

J.I. Packer says it this way:

> My present body — "brother ass," as Francis of Assisi would have me call it — is like a student's old jalopy; care for it as I will, it goes precariously and never very well and often lets me and my Master down. (Very frustrating!) But my new body will feel and behave like a Rolls-Royce, and then my service will no longer be spoiled.[2]

C.S. Lewis says they give you unimpressive horses to learn to ride on, and only when you are ready for it are you allowed an animal that will gallop and jump.[3]

What are these bodies like? Paul gives us a few clues.[4]

- They will be *imperishable* (verse 42), meaning that they will not wear out or grow old or be subject to sickness or disease. In our resurrection bodies we will see humanity as God intended it to be.
- Paul also says our bodies will be raised "*in glory*" (verse 43). This is contrasted with "dishonor," and is meant to convey beauty and attractiveness.
- Our bodies will be raised "*in power*" (verse 43), as opposed to the weakness of our current bodies. Don't think infinite power, like a super hero, but strength sufficient to do all that God asks of you.

---

2 Packer, *Affirming the Apostles' Creed*, 139.
3 Referenced in ibid., 139.
4 See Grudem, *Systematic Theology*, 831-832.

- This new body will be a "*spiritual body*" (verse 44). This doesn't mean a non-physical body, but a physical body raised to the degree of perfection for which God originally intended it.

Most importantly, *we shall be like Jesus*. John explains, "beloved, we are God's children now, and what we will be has not yet appeared; but we know that when he appears we shall be like him..." (I John 3:2). Paul adds, "the first man was from the earth, a man of dust; the second man is from heaven. As was the man of dust, so also are those who are of the dust, and as is the man of heaven, so also are those who are of heaven. Just as we have borne the image of the man of dust, we shall also bear the image of the man of heaven" (I Corinthians 15:47-49).

Stumbling Block for Some

For some people, the teaching of the resurrection of the body is a real stumbling block. This was the case even in Paul's time. The resurrection of the dead was just as hard to believe then as it is today. In verse 35, Paul anticipates objections to this teaching: "But someone will ask, 'how are the dead raised? With what kind of body do they come?'" Paul's response: "You foolish person!" (verse 36). This sounds pretty harsh, but Paul is exposing the doubt that drives his opponents' questions.

Paul is concerned here with the Corinthians' lack of imagination, their lack of awe at what God is going to do. They miss the forest for the trees. Rather than be astounded by the goodness of God in promising to bring about the redemption of our bodies, they quibble and speculate about details. How could the dead be raised? How could God do that? And if he were to do it, what would I look like? Would I look like I did at 18 or 80? Will I have my tooth fillings? Will I have a receding hairline? Paul has no patience with any of this. He says, "How foolish! You're missing the point."

A Matter For Worship

One who didn't miss the point was Emily Dickinson. She had a lifelong struggle with the great questions of the Christian faith. But in one poem she leaps across the terrain of doubt on a gust of joy, as one scholar puts it. She begins her poem by quoting Paul.

"And with what body do they come?" —
Then they *do* come — Rejoice!...
"Body!" Then *real* — a Face and Eyes —
to know that it is *them*!
Paul knew the Man that knew the News —
He passed through Bethlehem![5]

Paul's words in I Corinthians caught Dickinson's imagination and swept her away in joy. She responded appropriately — with praise and awe and worship.

5 Emily Dickinson, "And With What Body Do They Come?," ed. Thomas H. Johnson, *The Complete Poems of Emily Dickinson* (New York, NY: Back Bay Books, 1976), number 1492.

"*Body*," Paul says. That means it's a real resurrection! "To know that it is them," our actual loved ones, not abstractions, not symbols, not shadows, not ghosts, not spirits, not ideas, not vapors, but solid, concrete, tactile, real — with bodies, faces, eyes. We have this promise from God's Word. The resurrection of the dead isn't a fable or a ghost story. It is hope for every Christian.

THIS HOPE WILL CHANGE YOUR LIFE

If you believe this, it doesn't just affect your hope for the future. It changes the way you live now.

Rethinking Your Destiny

For one, you will begin to rethink your own destiny. Jesus says in John 5, "I tell you the truth, whoever hears my word and believes him who sent me has eternal life and will not be condemned, he has crossed over from death to life" (John 5:24). But the Bible teaches that when the trumpet sounds not everyone will delight in this resurrection — only those who "believe in him," those who "belong to Christ."

There are some places in the Bible that talk about a resurrection for all people, believers and non-believers alike. But for those who are not in Christ, this is a "resurrection of judgment."[6] Only those who have trusted in Christ as Savior, who are "in Christ," will rise with him forever.

Why is this the case? Because sin separates us from God, and only Christ can bridge the gap. "The sting of death is sin" (I Corinthians 15:56). This is what makes death so painful. Only in Jesus can the sting of death be taken away. Will you be part of the resurrection of believers at that trumpet blast? Is I Corinthians 15 describing your future?

In his book *The Problem of Pain*, C.S. Lewis writes of that day:

> All of your life an unattainable ecstasy has hovered just beyond the grasp of your consciousness. The day is coming when you will wake to find, beyond all hope, that you have attained it, or else, that it was within your reach and you have lost it forever.[7]

You don't want to lose it forever. But if you have trusted in Christ, you do not need to fear death. It has no sting because Christ has taken away the sin that separates us from God. Hoping in this truth will forever change your sense of your own destiny.

Living for Mission

Second, if you believe in the resurrection of the body, you will become more oriented toward God's mission. Paul wrote, "If the dead are not raised, 'Let us eat and drink, for tomorrow we die'" (I Corinthians 15:32). If the resurrection of the

---

6 See John 5:29, Acts 24:15, Matthew 25:31-46, Daniel 12:2.

7 C.S. Lewis, *The Problem of Pain* (San Francisco, CA: HarperOne, 2001), chap. 10.

body is not a reality, then you might as well do everything you can to maximize your pleasure, because it's all the pleasure and joy you will ever have. You should put yourself first. Get what you can in the here and now.

But if the resurrection of the dead is true, and if you really believe it, then you can live an entirely different kind of life. You can forego your own pleasure to serve other people, because you know your time now is just a blip compared to eternity. Knowing that the resurrection is your future enables you to take up your cross in the present, and live like Jesus, the one who laid his life down.

The Christian faith underwent amazing growth in the second and third centuries. In a period of about a hundred years, the church went from being 6-8 percent of the Roman Empire to almost 50 percent.[8] How did that happen?

During this time, two great plagues ravaged the empire. One was in AD 165, and the other in 251. They were awful and devastated cities throughout the region. At one point an estimated 35,000 people per week were dying in Rome.

No one was exactly sure how the plague was spread, but it was known that one could get it by contact. Because of this, when people started to get really sick, those who had the opportunity fled the city of Rome. The rich got out of town, because they had the means to do it. Even doctors fled in huge numbers. Families would abandon their kin.

This was true of everyone, save for one group: the Christians. The Christians stayed in large numbers, and they cared for those who came down with this disease. They cared for their own sick, but they also cared for the pagan sick. They risked their lives, and many were infected with the disease and died.

Why did the Christians stay while most of the pagan peoples left? It's not that Christians were naturally more courageous than the others. But, some historians believe it had to do with their worldview. Pagans had no assurance of the afterlife. Their religion was ambivalent about whether or not there was life after death. Most believed that this world was all there would be. Christians, on the other hand, knew this fallen world was the prelude to something more glorious; they believed in the resurrection of the dead. Thus, it makes sense that the Christians stayed and the pagans did not. If this life is all there is, you'd better not get the plague. But if you believed, like the Christians did, that you would one day be raised up, then you could face the plague in order to care for others. This point of doctrine, this belief, freed them up to live risky lives.

It turns out the death rate for someone with the plague was cut in half by simply having someone to care for them; regular food, drink, and comfort prolonged the sick person's life. The Christians survived at a much higher rate because their family and friends stayed to care for them. Many of the pagans were cared for by Christians, and many of those that survived became Christians.

Belief in the resurrection of the dead enables you to live a big life. It allows you to take up your cross and move toward pain and suffering. Those second

---

8 See Rodney Stark, *The Rise of Christianity: A Sociologist Reconsiders History.* (Princeton, NJ: Princeton University Press, 1996).

-century Christians knew that because of the resurrection death had lost its sting. They didn't have to be afraid.

The resurrection of the body also pushes Christians to care for physical needs as well as spiritual. If this doctrine teaches us anything, it's that the material world matters. God cares about the physical — so much so that he's going to raise physical bodies.

Abounding in the Work of the Lord

Finally, Paul concludes I Corinthians 15 by exhorting Christians to abound in the work of the Lord. Verse 58 begins with the word "therefore." "Therefore," in light of what I just told you about the resurrection, "my beloved brothers, be steadfast, immovable..." And how can you do that? You need to hope to be steadfast and immovable, a hope in the glorious eternity ahead. He continues, exhorting the Corinthians to be "always abounding in the work of the Lord, knowing that in the Lord your labor is not in vain." The work of the Lord is the proclamation of the gospel, going out and bearing fruit in cities and communities. This is the work the church is called to do.

How does belief in the resurrection of the body help you to do this work? For one thing, it enables you to give your life away to others, because you know this life is not all there is. But secondly, the resurrection of the dead teaches us that everyone we meet is facing one of two eternal destinies.

You have never met a mere mortal. C.S. Lewis writes in *The Weight of Glory*, "Next to the Blessed Sacrament itself, your neighbor is the holiest object presented to your senses."[9] Every person you meet has one of two eternal destinies ahead of them. May we have the strength to love the people around us, proclaiming the good news of a risen Christ who will raise others with him.

---

9 C.S. Lewis, *The Weight of Glory* (San Francisco, CA: HarperOne, 2001), 9.

STUDY QUESTIONS:

- What are some of the implications of knowing that the resurrection will involve glorified bodies and not just spirits?

- What might be a modern equivalent of the early church's moving into the cities to care for plague victims? How can you move toward the pain of others today? What will give you the courage?

- How can the teaching of the resurrection of the body give you more courage to live out God's mission?

- How does Emily Dickinson echo Paul in her response to unanswered questions about the precise nature of the resurrection of the body? How should you?

- If you really believed in the resurrection of the body, what would change about your life?

The Life Everlasting

CHAPTER 13

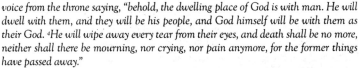

¹Then I saw a new heaven and a new earth, for the first heaven and the first earth had passed away, and the sea was no more. ²And I saw the holy city, new Jerusalem, coming down out of heaven from God, prepared as a bride adorned for her husband. ³And I heard a loud voice from the throne saying, "behold, the dwelling place of God is with man. He will dwell with them, and they will be his people, and God himself will be with them as their God. ⁴He will wipe away every tear from their eyes, and death shall be no more, neither shall there be mourning, nor crying, nor pain anymore, for the former things have passed away."

⁵And he who was seated on the throne said, "behold, I am making all things new." Also he said, "write this down, for these words are trustworthy and true." ⁶And he said to me, "it is done! I am the Alpha and the Omega, the beginning and the end. To the thirsty I will give from the spring of the water of life without payment. ⁷The one who conquers will have this heritage, and I will be his God and he will be my son. ⁸But as for the cowardly, the faithless, the detestable, as for murderers, the sexually immoral, sorcerers, idolaters, and all liars, their portion will be in the lake that burns with fire and sulfur, which is the second death."

²²And I saw no temple in the city, for its temple is the Lord God the Almighty and the Lamb. ²³And the city has no need of sun or moon to shine on it, for the glory of God gives it light, and its lamp is the Lamb. ²⁴By its light will the nations walk, and the kings of the earth will bring their glory into it, ²⁵and its gates will never be shut by day — and there will be no night there. ²⁶They will bring into it the glory and the honor of the nations. ²⁷But nothing unclean will ever enter it, nor anyone who does what is detestable or false, but only those who are written in the Lamb's book of life.

²²:¹Then the angel showed me the river of the water of life, bright as crystal, flowing from the throne of God and of the Lamb ²through the middle of the street of the city; also, on either side of the river, the tree of life with its twelve kinds of fruit, yielding its fruit each month. The leaves of the tree were for the healing of the nations. ³No longer will there be anything accursed, but the throne of God and of the Lamb will be in it, and his servants will worship him. ⁴They will see his face, and his name will be on their foreheads. ⁵And night will be no more. They will need no light of lamp or sun, for the Lord God will be their light, and they will reign forever and ever.

Revelation 21:1-8, 21:22 - 22:5

he week we worked on this chapter I (Josh) lost a friend. So the ideas of life, death, and eternity are very real and practical to me as I reflect on them. What does it mean to confess belief in the life everlasting with the Apostles' Creed? There is no better place to turn in the Scriptures than the last few chapters of the book of Revelation.

The picture the Apostle John gives us of the next world is significantly different from what many have come to believe. Some strains of Islam picture the world to come as a paradise where, as a heroic man, you will have 60 virgin companions to serve you.[1] In Buddhism, the goal is to end the cycle of suffering and to cease to exist all together. Hinduism teaches there is a continuous cycle of rebirth, and through karma, you either move up or down the chain of being; you might be reborn as a king or queen if you are good, or a rat or insect if you are bad. Mormonism imagines a heaven where you might be able to rule your own planet as a kind of mini-god. And pop-culture versions of Christianity picture heaven as this place where you dress in white, float around on a cloud all day, and learn to play the harp.

But the biblical picture of the life everlasting is quite different than all of these. Heaven exists right now, and if you are connected to Christ and die, you go there. Jesus says to the thief on the cross, "Today, you will be with me in paradise" (Luke 23:43). But there is a future world to come that God is going to bring about, and this new Jerusalem is what John is describing here. Literally, John says, heaven is going to come down and transform everything.

WHAT WE LONG FOR

This is good news, first, because we all have a sense that we were made for eternity. We have a longing inside us for another world.

C.S. Lewis says the very fact that every culture writes and thinks and philosophizes about heaven and eternity points to the fact that we are not made just for this world in its current condition. It's as if you were a marine biologist and you discovered a fish that had lungs. If you saw this, you'd conclude that somewhere along the way this fish had ancestors that breathed air. The very fact that we even imagine heaven speaks to the notion that we were made for another world.

In another place, Lewis writes, "Heaven is that remote music we are born remembering."[2] The whole human race has a kind of deep memory of paradise lost, a faint but powerful awareness that there must be another, better world for which we are better suited.

Not only do we have an internal sense of this, but we also have an outward longing for it. We have a sense that this world is not as it should be. We only have to read the newspapers and watch TV to see the suffering, sickness, and disease

---

1 For the record, this sounds like a lot better deal for the man than for the virgins.
2 Referenced by Michael R. Walker in a sermon titled "Heaven," at Highland Park Presbyterian Church, Dallas, TX, July 15, 2007.

that is all too pervasive in our world. These things might touch us personally — a sick child, a broken relationship, an obvious injustice. It makes us long for a different world. We know something is broken. We know things should be different.

My wife and I (Josh) have seen the band U2 on a couple of occasions. One of their standout songs is "I Still Haven't Found What I'm Looking For." When they first wrote this song, some Christians didn't know quite what to make of it. How could a band whose chief members are professing Christians sing "I still haven't found what I'm looking for"? If you have Jesus, what could you still be looking for?

It's meant to be a song about the Kingdom of God, which Christians still wait and watch for.

> I believe in the Kingdom Come
> Then all the colors will bleed into one
> Bleed into one
> But yes I'm still running
> You broke the bonds
> And you loosed the chains
> Carried the cross
> Of my shame
> Oh my shame
> You know I believe it
> But I still haven't found what I'm looking for[3]

Bono is looking for the Kingdom of God, but it's not here yet, at least not in its fullness. We long for the Kingdom. We long for the life everlasting. And John tells us that when it comes, it will be even better than we expect.

BETTER THAN WE EXPECT

The life everlasting will be so utterly different from our experience of the world now that it's hard to even wrap our minds around what it is going to be like. We might sometimes taste eternity, but those tastes are often overwhelmed by our awareness of our broken world.

Living in New Orleans, I (Ray) know what a whiplash life can be at every moment. We were recently at the final parade of the Mardi Gras season, an utterly lovely moment. I thought, "I don't know of a better picture of heaven than a Mardi Gras parade." It's a picture of grace and hospitality — everyone on the floats has paid a lot of money to give things away to strangers. This is the only major event like this I know of that is completely free of advertising or sponsorship. Nobody makes any money from it. They just get together to celebrate, and to give and to share. It's a picture of creativity that reflects our Creator. Its diversity is beautiful: all walks of life line up together to share, to talk, to laugh, to celebrate

---

3 U2. "I Still Haven't Found What I'm Looking For." *The Joshua Tree*. Island Records, 1987.

together. It is the best celebration I know, a glimpse of the party that is the Kingdom of God.

Then I got home and opened my laptop, and there were the pictures. People in their festive green and gold and purple helplessly crowded around a young man bleeding on the ground. He had been shot on the parade route half a mile from where my family and I had been standing.

In the midst of these almost otherworldly, joyous, wildly beautiful celebrations, there are signs of brokenness and death all around. As soon as the parade passes, you look behind you and see some of the 172,000 New Orleans homes that were flooded, some 50,000 still in ruins seven years later. Or you pick up the paper and read a report of yet another murder.

This is a reminder to us: all of our celebrations are marred by the fall. This is true in New Orleans, or Cincinnati, or any other place in our fallen world.

But these words from Revelation tell us that there is a different world coming: a perfect celebration, "tears wiped away, all things new." It's hard even to try and fit this picture into our grid of experience. How can there be a world made perfect? What will it look like? What will we do there?

John gives us a few characteristics of this eternal kingdom. First of all, it will constitute the restoration of this world.

The Restoration of This World

Revelation 21:1 says that there will be a new heavens and a new earth. There are a couple of different Greek words that get translated as "new" in the New Testament. The word here is *kainos*, which means new in the sense of *quality*, not in the sense of *time*.

Let's see if we can illustrate the difference. If I said, "I need new clothes," I'd be telling you that I need to get rid of my old clothes, and buy new ones. By saying "new," I mean they are new to me: new in terms of time. I didn't have them before, but I have them now. This is *not* the way John uses *kainos* here.

Now if I said, "I've been going to the gym lately. I've been eating right. I'm a new man," what I mean to say is not that the old me has been junked, but that I've been transformed. This is the kind of thing John means in describing a new heavens and a new earth, except he means it in a grander sense; it's a completely radical transformation.

You may have noticed these last few chapters in Revelation sound an awful lot like the first two chapters of the Bible. In the early chapters of Genesis we see the creation of the heavens and the earth. Here, we see the creation of a new heaven and a new earth. In the Garden of Eden, there is a river, and a tree of life. In the new Jerusalem, there is a garden in the middle of the city, and a river, and on the banks of the river is the tree of life. Genesis 3 tells the story of sin and death and curse. Revelation 20-22 tells us about redemption, life, and the blessing of God.

Do you see what John is doing? He is telling us the story of God's rehabilitation of the world. Revelation gives us a picture of God undoing the fall and evil and death and the curse.

At the end of *The Lord of the Rings*, Sam Gamgee discovers that his friend Gandalf is not dead, as he'd previously thought. He sees Gandalf and cries, "Is everything sad going to come untrue?"[4]

God is on a rehab mission. This has been his plan all along. He is making a new Kingdom, sometimes called the Kingdom of God, other times called the Kingdom of heaven. This Kingdom has already broken into the world with Jesus Christ's incarnation, but it will be consummated at the end when Jesus returns again. Everything sad is going to come untrue.

Romans 8:21-22 says "...the creation itself will be set free from its bondage to corruption and obtain the freedom of the glory of the children of God. For we know that the whole creation has been groaning together in the pains of childbirth until now." In the same way sin has affected us, corrupted us, and kept us from being all that we were created to be, God's creation has also been marred by sin. Somehow sin has thrown all creation out of whack, and the world is not as it should be.

In Romans 8 Paul pictures the created world, standing on its tip-toes, like a child waiting for a parade to start, looking for its liberation. When John says God is making a "new heaven and a new earth," he is writing about a liberation so transformative, so radical, that all the vestiges of corruption and decay will be burned away.

There is a really important application for us here. John tells us there will be a comprehensive renovation of this world. God is coming to redeem this world, not to abolish it.

Maybe you've heard the phrase, "If you're too heavenly minded, you're no earthly good." It suggests that those who focus on the life of the world to come do so at the expense of the present. This was John Lennon's criticism of religion in "Imagine."

> Imagine there's no Heaven
> It's easy if you try
> No hell below us
> Above us only sky
> Imagine all the people
> Living for today[5]

Lennon says that if you believe in heaven, you're going to forsake this world. You won't do anything for it. But we know better. God is coming to restore this world, not to junk it. It will be transformed, liberated, and made new, but not tossed away.

---

4 J.R.R. Tolkien, *The Return of the King*. Sally Lloyd-Jones makes great use of this line in her excellent children's Bible, *The Jesus Storybook Bible* (Grand Rapids, MI: ZonderKidz 2007).

5 John Lennon. "Imagine." *Imagine* (EMI, 1971).

God cares for his world so much that he is going to redeem it. One day there will be a new New Orleans, and a new Cincinnati, and they will be perfect and last forever. It is this notion that ought to drive us to care about mission in the here and now. We ought to care about people, that they might know God. But we also ought to care about neighborhoods and communities and justice and love and reconciliation. And as we pray, "Thy Kingdom come, thy will be done, on earth as it is in heaven," we pray the Kingdom down. We pull heaven down into the earth. We begin the work that Jesus will complete at the end, a new order.

A New Order

Revelation tells us that God will rid the world fully and finally of all infection and evil. This makes way for a new cosmic order where brokenness and suffering and death are banished. This is the substance of Revelation 21:4: "He will wipe away every tear from their eyes..." There will be rest from your trials, pain and enemies. "And death shall be no more, neither shall there be mourning, nor crying, nor pain anymore, for the former things have passed away." The new order will be characterized by peace and joy. None of the evils of the old world can hinder the saints from fully enjoying the consummate presence of God.

John was writing to comfort a people suffering intense persecution. His words are meant to grant them the hope to withstand their trials. When we think of our problems at work or school, we often say we're being thrown to the lions. Our lions are figurative, but for first-century Christians they were the real thing. Belief in the life everlasting was a living hope for people experiencing the most severe of troubles — how much more then for us! If you grasp this, you can face anything.

Several years ago my wife and I (Ray) went on a study program in Israel. Early in our trip, we went on a day-long hike to visit archaeological sites. We hiked all day through rough, rocky areas being beaten down by the arid climate. These were not the touristy spots, so there were no concession stands or restaurants around. All we had to eat the whole day was what we had remembered to pack. Somehow Kathy and I had missed that memo, and so all we had that day was what we could mooch off the others in our group. We were hiking in the heat for miles, dying of thirst and aching with hunger. All day, what kept me going was the thought of getting back to our room and getting a big plate of falafel and hummus, and an icy orange juice. The hike went on for 14 hours, but I could go on as long as I knew the orange juice was waiting for me back at the room. What sustained me was the hope of what would come after.

There are disappointments, broken dreams and broken hearts in the lives of people reading this book right now. You're not facing literal lions, but maybe you're exhausted, thirsty, thinking, "My marriage is so bad. I don't think I can take it much longer. Where can I get the strength to go on?" Or, "I don't think I can get out of bed and go to that job I hate one more day." You might be disheartened by the injustice you see around the country and in your city, or by the darkness of your own heart. Maybe you can't bear the loneliness that you feel, or you struggle with chronic pain and sickness. Where can you get strength for today?

It comes in the hope of a glorious future. You can try dieting; you can buy yourself a new iPad; you can switch jobs or cities or marriages or churches. You may escape the pain for a few moments. But in order to be sustained, you need a much bigger hope than any of those things can bring.

A new heavens and a new earth with a new order is coming. That knowledge is strength for the journey today. Frederich Nietzsche, who said a lot of wrong things, got it right when he said, "He who has a *why* to live for, can deal with almost any *how*."

God at the Center

But there is something else, something larger, separating our world from the one to come: God will be there. "Behold, the dwelling place of God is with man. He will dwell with them, and they will be his people, and God himself will be with them as their God" (Revelation 21:3). The best thing about the world to come is that God is going to dwell with us. This is the hope and fulfillment of the entire body of the Old Testament. This is what God's plan of redemption has always been driving for. God wants to live with his people.

ENTERING THE LIFE EVERLASTING

Sadly, John tells us that not everyone will be in the new Jerusalem. Though the thought might startle us, it shouldn't be surprising. The Kingdom of God is the environment of his glory. He will dwell with his people, and his presence will be the city's light. But some people spend their entire lives on earth running from God's presence. If eternal glory is mainly about dwelling with God, then they won't want to be there. And they won't be. John makes it clear that not everyone will enter into this heavenly city. "The one who conquers will have this heritage, and I will be his God and he will be my son. But as for the cowardly, the faithless, the detestable, as for murderers, the sexually immoral, sorcerers, idolaters, and all liars, their portion will be in the lake that burns with fire and sulfur, which is the second death" (Revelation 21:7-8).

This can be hard stuff to swallow. And John gives a list of things in verse 8 that will keep people from entering the city. It seems to be somewhat of an arbitrary list. He is not saying, "These are the worst sins, these are the ones that will keep you from heaven and send you to hell. Some other minor ones we'll overlook at the gate." John is simply listing common sins, and some that he's warned the people about at the beginning of Revelation in his letters to the seven churches. The list here is not meant to be exhaustive.

But ask yourself something: doesn't this make you a little nervous? Couldn't some of these things describe you, at least at some point in your life? Coward, liar, sexually immoral, faithless. Some of these words describe us.

If these are the people who don't get in, who does get in? Verse 7 tells us that it's "the conquerors." Some translations say the "over-comers." But who are they? Maybe you'd expect it to be the opposites of those people listed in verse 8. The cowards don't get in, so the brave must. The sexually immoral don't get in, so the morally pure must. Liars don't get in, so you'd better be honest.

But that's not what John says. Who are the conquerors? Who are the over-comers? Not the moral, not the upright, but *the thirsty*. "It is done! I am the Alpha and the Omega, the beginning and the end. To the thirsty I will give from the spring of the water of life without payment" (Revelation 21:6).

That is how you get into the world to come — by being thirsty, by asking God for something you cannot pay for. This is the gospel. If you get nothing else from this book, you must learn this. Salvation comes not by being moral, or right, or pure. In fact, the Bible says none of these things are true of any of us anyway. Rather, we get in on the life everlasting by recognizing we're not moral, we're not right, we're not pure. We get into the Kingdom of heaven because we are thirsty: for forgiveness, for mercy, for God's grace. We get in by recognizing that we are in need of a Savior. And by placing our faith in Jesus Christ, we drink the "spring of the water of life without payment."

C.S. Lewis closed his Narnia series like this. This is the last paragraph of *The Last Battle*:

> "There was a real railway accident," said Aslan softly. "Your father and mother and all of you are — as you used to call it in the Shadowlands — dead. The term is over: the holidays have begun. The dream is ended: this is the morning."
>
> And as He spoke He no longer looked to them like a lion; but the things that began to happen after that were so great and beautiful that I cannot write them. And for US this is the end of all the stories, and we can most truly say that they all lived happily ever after. But for THEM it was only the beginning of the real story. All their life in this world and all their adventures in Narnia had only been the cover and the title page: now at last they were beginning Chapter One of the Great Story, which no one on earth has read: which goes on for ever: in which ever chapter is better than the one before.[6]

"Eye has not seen, nor ear heard, neither has it entered the heart of man, the things God has prepared for them that love him" (I Corinthians 2:9). He never fails as we hope in his promises, particularly in his promise of the life everlasting.

---

6 C.S. Lewis, *The Last Battle* (San Francisco, CA: Harper Collins, 2000), 223.

STUDY QUESTIONS:

- Why should a belief that this world is eternal and will one day be renewed cause us to be more willing to serve our cities now?

- The promise of the coming new heaven and new earth brought real hope and action into the lives of John's original audience, the persecuted early church. In what way do you need this hope today? What should it do to you to embrace this hope more fully?

- It is not the moral ones who will live in the new heavens and the new earth; it is the thirsty (verse 6). Are you thirsty for the Kingdom?

Scripture Index

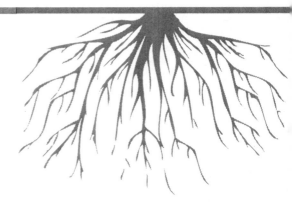

Bibliography & Works Cited

Books

Abbott, Edwin, *Flatland*. Oxford: Oxford University Press, 2006.

Barclay, William, *The Apostles' Creed*. Philadelphia, PA: Westminster John Knox Press, 1998.

Barth, Karl, *Church Dogmatics* IV/1 (tr. Geoffrey W. Bromiley). Edinburgh: Clark, 1956.

____ *Dogmatics in Outline*. San Francisco, CA: Harper and Row, 1959.

Begg, Alistair, *What the Angels Wish They Knew*. Chicago, IL: Moody Press, 1999.

Bell, Rob, *Love Wins*. New York: HarperOne, 2011.

____ *Velvet Elvis: Repainting the Christian Faith*. Grand Rapids, MI: Zondervan, 2005.

Boice, James Montgomery, *Psalms, Vol. 2*. Grand Rapids, MI: Baker Books, 1996.

Calvin, John, *The Acts of the Apostles, vol.1*. Grand Rapids, MI: Wm. B. Eerdmans, 1995.

____ *Institutes of the Christian Religion*. Philadelphia, PA: Westminster, 1960 [org. 1559].

Davies, Paul, *Superforce*. Austin, TX: Touchstone, 1984.

Driscoll, Mark, and Gerry Breshears, *Vintage Jesus: Timeless Answers to Timely Questions*. Wheaton, IL: Crossway Books, 2007.

Gordon, Ernest, *Through the Valley of the Kwai*. New York, NY: Wipf & Stock, 1997.

Gorman, Michael J., *Cruciformity*. Grand Rapids, MI: Wm. B. Eerdmans, 2001.

Grudem, Wayne, *Systematic Theology: An Introduction to Biblical Doctrine*. Grand Rapids, MI: Zondervan, 1994.

Guthrie, Nancy, *Come Thou Long-Expected Jesus: Experiencing the Peace and Promise of Christmas*. Wheaton, IL: Crossway, 2008.

Harris, Joshua, *Stop Dating the Church*. Sisters, OR: Multnomah, 2004.

James, P.D., *Original Sin*. New York, NY: Warner, 1994.

Johnson, Luke Timothy, *The Creed: What Christians Believe and Why it Matters*. New York, NY: Doubleday, 2003.

Keller, Timothy, *The Reason for God: Belief in the Age of Skepticism*. New York, NY: Dutton, 2009.

Kuhn, Thomas, *The Structure of Scientific Revolutions*. Chicago, IL: University of Chicago Press, 1996.

Larson, Bruce and Keith Miller, *The Edge of Adventure*. Waco, TX: Word Books, 1983.

Lewis, C.S., *The Last Battle*. New York, NY: HarperCollins, 1984.

____ *The Screwtape Letters*. San Francisco, CA: HarperCollins, 2001.

____ *The Problem of Pain*. San Francisco, CA: HarperOne, 2001

____ *The Weight of Glory*. San Francisco, CA: HarperOne, 2001.

Lloyd-Jones, Sally, *The Jesus Storybook Bible*. Grand Rapids, MI: ZonderKidz, 2007.

Machen, J. Gresham, *The Virgin Birth of Christ*. New York, NY: Harper & Brothers, 1930.

McGrath, Alister E., *Christian Theology: An Introduction*. New York, NY: Wiley-Blackwell, 2001.

____ *"I Believe": Exploring the Apostles' Creed*. Downer's Grove, IL: IVP Books, 1998.

Morgenau, Henry and Roy Abraham Varghese, eds., *Cosmos, Bios, and Theos*. La Salle, IL: Open Court, 1992.

Orr, James, *The Virgin Birth of Christ*. New York, NY: Charles Scribner's Sons, 1907.

Ortberg, John, *The Life You Always Wanted*. Grand Rapids, MI: Zondervan, 2002.

Packer, J.I., *Affirming the Apostles' Creed*. Wheaton, IL: Crossway, 2008.

Piper, John, *Desiring God*. Sisters, OR: Multnomah, 1986.

____ *Let the Nations be Glad*. Grand Rapids, MI: Baker Academic, 2003.

____ *The Pleasures of God*. Sisters, OR: Multnomah, 1991.

Putnam, Robert, *Bowling Alone: The Collapse and Revival of American Community*. New York, NY: Simon & Schuster, 2001.

Spurgeon, Charles H., *Morning and Evening: A New Edition of the Classic Devotional Based on the Holy Bible* (Alistair Begg, ed.). Wheaton, IL: Crossway, 2003.

Stark, Rodney, *The Rise of Christianity: A Sociologist Reconsiders History.* Princeton, NJ: Princeton University Press, 1996.

Stott, John R.W., *The Message of Ephesians.* Downers Grove, IL: InterVarsity Press, 1986.

Tolkien, *The Return of the King: Being the third part of the Lord of the Rings,* (Boston: Houghton Mifflin Company, 1999), p. 930.

Turner , Steve, *Nice and Nasty.* London: Marshall, Morgan, and Scott, 1980.

Van Harn, Roger E., *Exploring and Proclaiming the Apostles' Creed.* Grand Rapids, MI: Wm. B. Eerdmans, 2004.

Volf, Miroslav, *Exclusion and Embrace.* Nashville, TN: Abingdon, 1996.

Walsh, Brian, and Sylvia Keesmaat, *Colossians Remixed: Subverting the Empire.* Downer's Grove, IL: IVP, 2004.

Wood, Ralph, *The Comedy of Redemption: Christian Faith and Comic Vision in Four American Novelists.* South Bend, IN: Univ. of Notre Dame Press, 1991.

Wright, N.T., *The Resurrection of the Son of God.* Minneapolis, MN: Fortress Press, 2003.

___ *Simply Christian: Why Christianity Makes Sense.* New York, NY: HarperOne, 2006.

Wright, N.T., and Marcus Borg, *The Meaning of Jesus: Two Visions.* San Francisco, CA: HarperOne, 2007.

Zacharias, Ravi, *Can Man Live Without God?* Nashville, TN: Thomas Nelson, 1994.

Articles / Statistics

"Hell is for Other People," *The Atlantic Monthly* (http://www.theatlantic.com/past/docs/issues/2004/01/primarysources.htm).

International Justice Mission (http://www.ijm.org/ourwork/injusticetoday).

"Men Met in Hotel Lobbies," *Washington Post* (June 16, 1901).

Leithart, Peter, "Christian Novelty: What Homer Could Not See, & Jane Austen Could," in *Touchstone* (Vol. 18, No. 2, March 2005).

Prager, Dennis, "The Sin of Forgivness," *The Wall Street Journal* (December 15, 1997).

Simic, Charles, "Down There on a Visit," *New York Times Review of Books* (Vol. 51, No. 13; Aug 12, 2004).

Trueman, Carl, "Thank God for Bandit Country," *Reformation 21,* June 2009 (http://www.reformation21.org/counterpoints/wages-of-spin/thank-god-for-bandit-country.php).

Sermons / Lectures

Davis, Andy, "Glory to God, the Creator," at First Baptist Church, Durham, NC: sermon, May 2, 2004.

Edwards, Jonathan, "A Divine and Supernatural Light," at Northampton, 1734 (http://www.monergism.com/thethreshold/articles/onsite/edwards_light. html).

Keller, Timothy, "Made for Relationship" at Redeemer Presbyterian Church, New York, NY, October 29, 2000.

____ "Who is the Spirit?" at Redeemer Presbyterian Church, New York, NY, July 4, 2010.

Piper, John, "Lessons From An Inconsolable Soul," at the Desiring God Pastor's Conference, Bethlehem, MN, February 2, 2010.

Walker, Michael R., "Heaven," at Highland Park Presbyterian Church, Dallas, TX, July 15, 2007.

Willson, Sandy, "Jesus Christ, the Glory of the Church" at Second Presbyterian Church, Memphis, TN, May 16, 1999.

Songs / Cultural References

Lennon, John, "Imagine." *Imagine*, EMI, 1971.

Phillips, Emo, "The Wisdom of Emo Phillips" (http://cmgm.stanford.edu/-lkozar/ EmoPhillips.html).

Indelible Grace, *The Hymn Sing: Live in Nashville*, Indelible Grace Music, 2010.

U2, "I Still Haven't Found What I'm Looking For" on *The Joshua Tree*. Island Records, 1987.

Webb, Derek, "The Church." *She Must and Shall Go Free*, INO Records, 2003.

Wesley, Charles, "Christ the Lord is Risen Today" (1739).

Police Women of Cincinnati. Relativity Television, 2011.

Acknowledgements

As we mentioned in the Preface, there are many whose help with this project through the years made it possible — and without them, this book wouldn't be before you.

We are deeply grateful for Matt Brown, pastor of Resurrection Presbyterian Church in Brooklyn, NY; Marty Garner, a member of Redeemer New Orleans; and Kristin Boys, a member of New City Cincinnati. Each of you contributed to this project in different, but vital, ways. Thank you.

We are also grateful for those who thought, taught, and wrote about the Apostles' Creed long before we did, whose wisdom and understanding were vital in the development of this book. Particularly (again, repeating ourselves from the Preface), we extend our thanks to Luke Timothy Johnson, Alister McGrath, and Roger Van Harn.

About the Authors

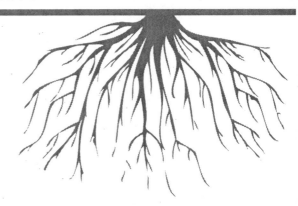

Rev. Dr. Raymond F. Cannata

Ray received his education at Wake Forest (B.A.), Princeton Theological Seminary (M.Div. and Th.M.) and Westminster Theological Seminary (D.Min.). He is currently senior pastor of Redeemer Presbyterian Church, a newer church plant for the Uptown neighborhood of New Orleans. His congregation has been helping to rebuild homes in New Orleans for over seven years and counting, and has worked on over 400 houses so far. Ray's work has been featured on many national television programs (*Anderson Cooper 360* and *Fox and Friends*), and magazines (*Paste, World*, etc.). He has taught doctoral classes on urban ministry at Covenant Theological Seminary. A major documentary film has been made about his quest to eat at every non-chain restaurant in his city (742 of them): *The Man Who Ate New Orleans*. He is an active member of the Mardi Gras club, the Krewe of the Rolling Elvi. He is married to Kathy and has two children, Andrew and Rachel.

Rev. Joshua D. Reitano

Joshua received his education at Miami University (B.S. and M.A.) and Princeton Theological Seminary (M.Div.). He is currently the lead pastor of New City Presbyterian Church, a congregation committed to changing lives and urban renewal in Cincinnati. He is a pastor in the Presbyterian Church in America and a member of the Acts 29 Church Planting Network. Joshua loves all things Cincinnati, especially Skyline Chili, Graeter's Ice Cream, and the Reds and Bengals. Unlike Ray, he's never had a documentary made about his life. However, he was an extra on the short-running *Daytona Beach* (a *Baywatch* spinoff starring Lee Majors). Joshua is married to Paige and they have a young daughter, Lucy.

About Doulos Resources

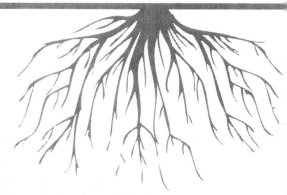

Our goal is to provide resources to support the church and kingdom, and to build up and encourage the pastors and leaders within the church. Our resources follow the model of Ephesians 4:12 — "to prepare God's people for works of service, so that the body of Christ may be built up." We produce books, curricula, and other media resources; conduct research to advance our goals; and offer advice, counsel, and consultation. We are Reformed and Presbyterian, but not exclusively so; while we do not lay aside our theological convictions, we believe our resources may be useful across a broader theological and ecclesiastical spectrum.

Our goal with *Rooted* as with all of our resources, is to offer well-edited, high-quality, and useful materials at an affordable price that makes our resources accessible to congregations and members of the church.

If you are interested in ordering additional copies of *Rooted*, or to order other materials that Doulos Resources offers, please visit our website (listed below). If you are ordering in quantity for a church or other ministry, contact us to inquire about a discount for quantity orders.

Doulos Resources Contact Information:

Telephone:
(901) 201-4612

Internet:
website: www.doulosresources.org
e-mail: info@doulosresources.org

Print/Digital Copies of
ROOTED

A t Doulos Resources, we've found that we often appreciate owning both print and digital editions of the books we read; perhaps you have found this as well. In our gratitude to you for purchasing a print version of this book, we are pleased to offer you free copies of the digital editions of *Rooted: the Apostles' Creed*. To obtain one or more of these, simply visit our eStore (estore.doulosresources.org) and enter the following discount code during checkout:

RootedDigitalDiscount

If you purchased a digital edition, you may use the same discount code to receive a discount deducting the full price of your digital edition off of the purchase price for a print edition.

Thank you for your support!

CPSIA information can be obtained
at www.ICGtesting.com
Printed in the USA
FFOW05n1745190815